'A breath-taking piece of work: and gripping as any novel, but u Rosenfeld's clear-eyed psychoanalytical honesty, also deeply consoling. I don't think writers – or human beings – can share their experience more movingly and generously than this.' – **Julie Myerson**

'A brave and beautifully written account of an experience usually shrouded in silence. This is such an intelligent and honest book.' – **Amelia Gentleman**

'Juliet's memoir is a tale of two losses: the loss of a partner and the loss of faith in the power of psychoanalysis to make soothing sense of trauma.' – *Daily Mail*

'I relate deeply to Juliet Rosenfeld's poignant account of the loss of her beloved. Death, while it awaits us all, remains the last taboo. I applaud Juliet's ability to fearlessly examine spousal loss and provide a roadmap for others who, one day, hope to navigate it with courage and grace.' – **Katie Couric**

'A masterpiece. I truly wish no one ever had to endure such a loss, but we are human beings and this is part of the deal. This book will be of help to everyone who reads it.' – **Professor Brett Kahr, Psychotherapist, Senior Fellow at Tavistock**

'I couldn't put it down… highly recommend.'
– **Heather Saul**, *Independent*

'Profound, insightful and moving, *The State of Disbelief* takes the reader on an honest and heartbreaking journey. With extraordinary talent, Juliet Rosenfeld articulates the unspeakable feelings each of us confront when faced with the loss of those we love. She gives words to our deepest and most lonely experiences, and by doing, helps us to process them. This is a powerful book that reminds us what it means to be human.'
– **Galit Atlas Ph.D., author of** *Emotional Inheritance*

'In this brilliant and deeply moving memoir, Juliet Rosenfeld turns to the writing of Sigmund Freud to help her find her way after unfathomable loss. *The State of Disbelief* is a beautifully crafted book of extraordinary power: about grief, mourning, and how we can all live more fully every day.' – **Will Schwalbe,** *New York Times* **bestselling author of** *The End of Your Life Book Club*

'Rarely has the physical nature of memory of the dead been so well written about.' – **The Oldie**

'This powerfully written book has much to say both to the bereaved and to those working with them about loss and how we can come to live with it, lovingly, as we once lived with the one who has died.' – *Therapy Today Magazine*

'Movingly captures the sheer weight of mourning in the lives of those left behind.' – **Beth Guilding,** *Times Literary Supplement*

'Love is a strange word to use about a book on bereavement, but the unflinching honesty of *The State of Disbelief* shines a light on the parts of life most of us would rather not - dying, bereavement and survival - and you feel stronger for reading it.' – **Lisa Armstrong,** *The Telegraph*

The State of Disbelief

Juliet Rosenfeld

To protect the privacy of others, some names and events have been changed, characters composited and incidents condensed.

First published in 2020 by Short Books
an imprint of Octopus Publishing Group Ltd
Carmelite House, 50 Victoria Embankment
London, EC4Y 0DZ
www.octopusbooks.co.uk
www.shortbooks.co.uk

An Hachette UK Company
www.hachette.co.uk

This expanded paperback edition published in 2022

10 9 8 7 6 5 4 3 2 1

A CIP catalogue record for this book is available from the British Library.

ISBN: 978-1-78072-544-4

Cover design by Jo Walker

Printed and bound in Great Britain by Clays Ltd, Elcograf S.p.A.

This FSC® label means that materials used for the product have been responsibly sourced

MIX
Paper from
responsible sources
FSC® C104740

AIR 27.04.62 – 08.02.15

We are never so defenceless against suffering as when we love, never so forlornly unhappy as when we have lost our love object or its love.

'Mourning and Melancholia'
Sigmund Freud, 1917

Contents

Afterword

Foreword

I am a psychotherapist and a widow. I experienced a brutal bereavement five years ago which devastated me and changed the course of my life completely. My husband Andrew, aged 51, a handsome, confident businessman, was diagnosed with lung cancer in an airless room high above the Marylebone Road on the Thursday before Christmas Eve, 2013. He had never smoked a cigarette. There was a dark view of skeleton treetops in Regent's Park, and the evening rush-hour traffic filed past determinedly as we were told the news by a locum GP, who we had met five minutes beforehand.

He died on 8th February 2015.

His sudden and unexpected death affected many people, terribly, in different ways; his parents, his adored first family. The only story of bereavement anyone can tell is their own, and no one can guess how a death made another person feel. This is only my story. But Andrew was a deeply loved son, brother and father, who lived for his four children.

Just as there is no hierarchy of grief, so to generalise about the experience would be a mistake, for sudden bereavement at the closest of quarters offers only two guarantees – firstly, it is idiosyncratic and secondly, completely unimaginable until it happens. My only conclusion is that who you are, and what you have already lived through, define your experience of bereavement.

As time passed I realised I had been left in the unusual position of having the tools to explore this experience through the framework of psychotherapy, psychoanalytic ideas and writing. I thought I would try to merge the clinical skills I have developed over the last decade treating patients in private practice and the NHS, alongside twelve years of five-times-a-week psychoanalysis, with an account of what close bereavement does to your mind. In our case, a terrifying illness appeared one day, out of the blue, and suddenly became terminal, resulting in Andrew's death, fourteen months after diagnosis. I wanted to describe this traumatic loss from a personal perspective by using the theoretical training that I had long used clinically.

But the truth is also that I wrote, to begin with, because there was no other option, no other way of making sense of an overwhelming feeling of disbelief about what was happening.

The experience of bereavement has left me with a deep interest in grief and mourning. It took me a while to realise how different these two feelings are, and how helpful an understanding of that difference can be. I wanted to capture these states of mind, and try to explain them in a way that is potentially therapeutic.

Central to this book is a short paper published in 1917

by Sigmund Freud, the founding father of psychoanalysis and psychotherapy. I rediscovered my scribbled-on and folded photocopy of 'Mourning and Melancholia' in the days after Andrew died, and it became a handmaid to my recovery. Poignantly, I found it in his bedside table. I wonder if he read it. I returned to it often, and kept it, talismanic, by my bed or on the desk in my consulting room.

Only seventeen pages long, 'Mourning and Melancholia' was written as World War I raged in 1915, and remained unpublished for two years. It is, like much of Freud's work, clinically original and innovative, but there is more to it than that. When I reread it in those first weeks I was struck by how it spoke to me, a century after its publication, when nothing else made any sense. Freud set out to define an idea that had been greatly preoccupying him; the effect of loss on the mind. He identified two distinct effects of loss: depression, (then known as melancholia) and mourning, which I term bereavement – and which he separated into two phases – grief and mourning.

This crucial distinction is what helped me to understand my own feelings: the savage trauma of loss that occurs at the moment of death – grief – and the longer, unpredictable evolution of that loss into something that we call mourning. Think of this as the earthquake and the after-shocks. The first is a shattering, visible, sudden eruption, which leaves the landscape devastated. The latter phase is slower, less predictable but just as painful, with occasional flashes back to the original grief. Ultimately, however, the wreckage is gradually cleared. The original shape of the terrain is visible. But the landscape is never the same again.

So, this is an explanation and differentiation of grief and mourning. For they are fundamentally *different* emotions, the latter only reachable after the former in some way departs. This discrepancy, not usually acknowledged, is part of the problem that the bereaved encounter. Grief today is often erroneously considered, as interchangeable with mourning. Contrary to some theorists and writers, I do not believe one can *work through* grief, in the same way one can work through other complicated experiences. To suggest it is possible risks a grave misunderstanding of the experience of the bereaved person. 'Working through' grief implies agency. Certainly in the consulting room (and outside it) the patient must work through the wished-for or unwished-for ending of a relationship, the loss of a job, a partner's anger, a parent's inadequacy, a bodily self-hatred, but not the grief brought on by a death. I had no role or part to play in Andrew contracting terminal cancer, and could take no responsibility for it (unlike, say, the ending of my first marriage, or my tendency to blame my parents or my feeling negatively judged by my analyst when I was late for a session). But grief is firmly in control and must be endured. If the conditions permit, it will find its own way elsewhere eventually – while mourning feels like it will never quite leave home, but must be accommodated in some way, for ever.

Reminding myself of these differing states of mind

kept me afloat in those early days, and reassured me that I might not descend into an unmanageable psychological breakdown.

'Mourning and Melancholia' is arguably Freud's finest work, moving between the conscious and unconscious consequences of loss in its many guises. Freud's genius was to recognise which symptoms are shared by the bereaved and the depressed. In essence, Freud states that in depression we do not often understand *why* we are depressed, as we do not know what has been lost, while in grief and mourning we know precisely what is gone. Yet this knowledge doesn't necessarily hasten the recovery.

My understanding of degrees of bereavement has grown greatly in the last five years, clinically, theoretically and of necessity personally. My grandparents died in their eighties, and a very close childhood friend was killed in a car crash during our teens. These experiences were so different – my grandparents' deaths sad but expected; the death of my sixteen-year-old friend shocking, and unbelievable for a while – but before Andrew died, I don't think I had any idea what this closest type of bereavement would feel like.

Death is a ubiquitous life experience and yet we pretend it will not affect us – until that choice is taken away. I wish we could, and believe we should talk more about death and bereavement, be more alive to it in life. After Andrew's death, in a state of shock, I went back to work with my patients and functioned well enough, but still struggled to conceptualise what his death was doing to my mind. During this period I decided to give up my further psychoanalytic training and developed a mistrust of my analyst, indeed lost faith in the process of psychoanalysis to help me. For a while, my own long psychoanalysis became a casualty of my very resistant strain of grief. The five-sessions-a-week treatment fell down badly six months or so after Andrew's death, and eventually ground to a standstill a year later, ten years into it. Generalisation is the antithesis of psycho-analytic thinking but I would not prescribe five-times-a-week analysis on the couch to my freshly bereaved self again. I would not wish my demanding, rigid first analyst on my shell-shocked self again, but who knows how it might have worked for someone else? Analysis is a most individual experience. I respect his earlier work with me and I have much to thank him for. I am still an admirer and exponent of psychoanalysis, not a critic, but I also believe that where possible telling the truth is fundamental to the discipline – and the truth is that psychoanalysis for grief did not work for me.

When, three years or so after Andrew's death, I began to distinguish between grief and mourning, I returned to psychoanalysis, although with a new analyst. From that point on, and with the help of this clinician, who was honest and wise but also kind, I learnt that mourning could mean a partial recovery of Andrew, mad though that sounds. I found I had returned to a liveable, and often enjoyable, life. It does not mean that I do not, still, miss him profoundly.

And as the new analysis began to work, I found

my own clinical work changing, that I was working in a much more confident way. One silver lining of this tragedy was that I found I wanted to (and could) work with patients where bereavement was a significant reason for coming to see a therapist. I knew – and I will always know – what they were talking about.

Lastly, this is the only opportunity I will have to say how much I loved Andrew, and how profoundly happy we were, even as the tumour refused to go quietly. Five years on, I have found, sometimes disconcertingly, that my love continues to survive his death. There is, of course, a price to be paid for this. It frustrates me at times that I cannot forget him, cannot move on completely and pretend that I never knew this man. Yet the idea I could forget him is devastating. This common paradox merits further examination, just as Freud's ideas, so central to this book, deserve a wider audience.

Juliet Rosenfeld, London, September 2019

Part I

1

Writing and Death

Ours was a second marriage for us both, unbearably and unimaginably cut short. We met in 2011 and he died four years later. I had no idea how exquisitely brief the time between our wedding and his funeral would be, just seven months.

Our years together are now exceeded by the years since his death but I still feel grateful that I knew him. This is the mourning, now well under way, still occasionally flooring me, leaving me feeling cheated and incensed at our bad fortune but also not. On good days now, I generally feel a sense of great luck that we had the time together that we did. I still also feel angry with him, for not being here, and for deserting me. Disappointingly, and I am reluctant to admit it, there are still days when I cry and cannot understand how he is no longer alive.

As I have started to comprehend more about what happened, I have understood why it took such a long time to write this book. I did not at first write about events; I wrote about what it felt like and what it did to my mind, which was to traumatise my thoughts. Trauma is proof to a human being that our most primitive and universally held fears can actually happen. A trauma fuels those earliest anxieties that we are alone in chaos with no one to keep us from the abyss. Trauma consequently takes its time to process and holds us back, static and stuck in the moment. For months I was horribly stuck in the moment of his death, as well as in the weeks leading up to that unimaginable half-hour.

I began writing three days before he died. I had to get words on paper that I could not say. The writing was private proof to me that something had happened and I wrote to check if I was still alive, and to keep Andrew alive in some way – at least to begin with. It was a way to keep him with me, for a little while longer. It was as if he had appeared and disappeared, overnight.

I always felt he approved of my writing about him; I discovered as I went through all his possessions that he had kept every scrappy note, and jotted Post-It as well as all the cards, letters, cartoons and idiotic rhymes I had ever sent him. As he understood and accepted me so completely in life, so he would understand my need to record the despair, anger and chaos that followed his death.

Bereavement has a unique position in the human lexicon of suffering and yet remains an impoverished subject of discussion – like death. Quite reasonably, no one wants to think about it much. The possibility of losing the person we love most dearly is not a conscious daily thought for most of us. The death of a lover (setting aside the death of a child, much less usual, and the most awful of losses) is too frightening to contemplate. So we don't. I certainly didn't.

Many of us will outlive a partner, although statistically, after a long life together, and with luck, having enjoyed a loving relationship or marriage. We vaguely (perhaps) anticipate these kinds of deaths at some point in the distant future. The very lucky may even be able to talk of their partner having had a 'good death', be left years of memories and feel a gratitude for what was enjoyed together. This does not mean that someone does not experience grief or mourning after a long partnership, but it can balance the shock of the absence. In cases where a long illness or frailty has meant that someone's quality of life is compromised, there can also be a feeling that it was 'time' for them to go.

The truth too is that death from 'natural causes' in very old age lacks tragedy, and while we cannot generalise, a 'good innings', or a 'life well lived' is compensation for most of those close to the deceased. But when death comes along very unexpectedly, and suddenly, in someone young, or youngish, and obliterates or sharply retracts a future, the experience is different.

Now, years after Andrew's death, I know that as the memory of intense happiness fades, so does the chronic pain. The Romanian philosopher Emil Cioran says, *Continuing to live is possible only because of the deficiencies of our imagination and our memories.* As the months and years pass, I realise that I am losing the sharpness of what it was like when Andrew was alive. Time has edited and blurred memories. I can no longer quite remember the contented context in which we lived. Death mixes the banal with the epic, the awesome with the ordinary. We are programmed to forget a lot of detail. Life would be impossibly painful if we remembered everything. One of the ways in which we overcome the death of a deeply loved person is by forgetting them.

But it is not just time that dims the past.

The absence of externalised ways of mourning means that accounts and memoirs have taken on an increasingly important role. Nowadays, we are often encouraged to talk about the dead person, to seek different sorts of therapeutic help, or join groups or online communities of strangers suffering similar loss. But writing allows for a different, private and more fundamental experience. In the aftermath of sudden or unexpected death, writing creates a unique space to describe the experience of the person you love dying, not least because you are still bound up with them, still have an active relationship with them that has suddenly, dramatically changed shape. Adam Phillips, the psychoanalyst, commented in an interview about bereavement at the Freud Museum in 2018 that death is back on the agenda, and people want to know more about it. But Phillips also says that what the living want most is not how-to guides, but personal accounts of the lived experience that are as honest and revealing as possible, about this strange and yet universal experience.

Naturally, in the various realms of academia, theology, medicine and psychiatry, there is plenty of writing about bereavement – and in psychoanalytic literature a great deal. But for the ordinarily curious reader, there isn't much, although some excellent memoirs have been written in the last few years – *The Iceberg* by Marion Coutts (2014), Kate Grosse's *Late Fragments* (2015), Paul Kalinithi's posthumous *When Breath Becomes Air* (2016) are very fine examples. I had read CS Lewis's exquisite *A Grief Observed* (1961), Ruth Picardie's *Before I Say Goodbye* (1997), John Diamond's *C: Because Cowards Get Cancer Too* (1999), as well as Joan Didion's *The Year of Magical Thinking* (2005), years before Andrew's death. These are defining and original accounts by literary writers which I enjoyed and was moved by as a reader, but did not return to as a griever. Partly because I stopped reading, a common symptom of grief. In addition, I could not watch television or go to the cinema for around six months. It was if I could not retain the beginning of a sentence or hold a whole paragraph in my mind, or remember a plot.

Had I been able to read would I have found these helpful? Each experience was so personal, relevant, articulate and resolved, that I could not then equate them with the nightmare in which I found myself.

The most commonly cited model of the knowledge of impending death and later, its application to bereavement, is that described by the psychiatrist Elizabeth

Kübler-Ross in her books *On Death and Dying* (1969) and *On Grief and Grieving* (2005). Hundreds of thousands of people have been helped by her writing and I was often referred to it by well-meaning friends. Kübler-Ross, from her work with terminally ill patients, defined five stages – denial, anger, bargaining, depression and finally acceptance, sometimes known as DABDA. She herself was clear that the stages were flexible, non-linear and not to be taken as a formula, but her work was not always interpreted in this way. Her stance was that patients with serious illnesses are often very sure they are dying and actually want those around them to acknowledge this, to be able to bear the process alongside them. This did not ring true for me. Firstly, Andrew, I believe, had no conscious idea of his own impending death and did not want to think or talk about it. And, bizarrely, now I think, no doctor told us it was even a remote possibility, or if they thought they did, the communication was lost, barred by the defensive mechanism at work between Andrew and me. Kübler-Ross's ideas created a paradigm shift 50 years ago in the treatment of the terminally ill, but before she died she stated that her notion of a journey either to death or through grief had been taken up in too simplistic or orderly a way.

And this is a problem. For we require neatness, tidiness and understanding in most areas of our lives, yet death often possesses the opposite characteristics. Kübler-Ross's model of the Five Stages of Grief made death sound controllable, manageable and systematic. My experience was that it was messy, unboundaried and incomprehensible in every possible way.

Equally, we have dispensed with many of the ritualised ways of signifying bereavement to those around us. I did not wear black for a year after Andrew died, stop the clocks or hang a wreath of yew on my front door. I followed Jewish traditions in the first week, and concerning his burial, but these were quickly over. I did gradually (and with the help of a kind rabbi) find private religious rituals of my own, but the external evidence of my state of mind was rapidly hidden. Grief nowadays goes unseen, and unchecked.

The narrative arc of this book is of course that of Andrew's illness, but not overtly. It would have been impossible not to revisit this experience, and it was a story I wanted to tell, but others have written in a much more informed way about cancer. I merely chart the chronological progression of the disease which was inevitable. Had we read the statistics we would have known this, but denial meant we did not. And while the disease adhered to the time frame set out by predetermined and painfully accurate meta-samples of other sufferers and their cancers, my mind did not.

Creativity is not generally an end in itself but rather a need to represent the truth as the creator sees it. The book is written in the past and the present, and the account of Andrew's last few weeks was written in the days and weeks after he died. The confused tenses convey how mystified I was about what was happening. As he began to die, I truly was *in* a state of disbelief. And as in my wayward psychological journey, nothing was linear. I took up the writing and dropped it and took it up again after Andrew's death, partly as I had to get back to my clinical work and rebuild my practice but also because I went through periods of having almost no thoughts, other than a complete and wholesale preoccupation with Andrew, to the exclusion of everything else – a curious state of mind. I was filled right up to the brim with him, like a too-full glass of water whose surface tension cannot be broken by movement for fear of spilling it.

I think now that this is what grief means: an acutely painful obsessive enmeshment with the person who has died and yet is fiendishly alive in your mind. Like bashing your head relentlessly against a wall, perhaps, or constant picking at a woody scab to make it bleed. It was a deeply unpleasant feeling and I was angry and troubled during the long months of the first two years, wounded, unable to be anaesthetised, because no drug could do what I needed it to do, which was to make me forget him, and return him. I wanted him gone and I wanted him back with equal fervour. At times it was unbearable, and as a consequence my mood was generally low and frustrated. It was often unfathomable to me, so how hard it must have been for the small but loving group around me – my parents, my cousins, my brother and several very close friends upon whom I felt totally reliant. A patient in my consulting room recently described 'walking on eggshells' around his newly widowed son, and I wanted to tell him he was not alone. I was livid with my parents for letting Andrew die, as my mother exasperatedly, but kindly explained to me one day. (You need your parents to protect you from horror whether you are six or 46, and they had failed.)

And it was only after the first three years that I finally began to see the grief yield space to its younger, more hopeful, sometimes problematic, but also loving sibling, mourning. This was a turning point, and a relief, and the writing began again.

2

Aftermath, Spring 2015

I will come back to what happened before 8th February, the day Andrew died. I remember waking up early one Sunday weeks later in our house in the country, and looking out at the fields beyond our garden wall and, suddenly, catastrophically knowing he was not there, would never ever be there again. I found myself on the floor seconds later, I can't recall how, next to the hem of the curtains, and I remember my chest struggling for breath; I was not crying but I could not call for help and I could not stand up. I was on the floor for an hour or maybe more. So strange. How did it end? Did I stand up again and go into my bathroom and look in the mirror, examine my still night-creased face, brush my teeth, wet a flannel? I have no memory of how I came out of that tearless, dry-land drowning that day.

For now I can say that I never lost my mind (even if I lost much of my life) from that day onwards. As a clinician I am sure of this. I do, however, think I went mad with grief, which theoretically I understood, and had seen in the consulting room, but never experienced. I don't mean mad in a psychiatric sense – although at times I did not know who I was – but mad in a psychoanalytic sense, on occasion. This did not go as far as what clinically would be called a 'psychotic break', when talking about a patient's state of mind. My madness lacked a dissociative quality (which is what satisfies the 'break'.) In other words, I did not lose touch with reality, though I did believe in phenomena that weren't evidence-based, as I will go on to describe. I remained conscious of time and place and I was also clear – as clear as it is possible to be about something so confusing – that the madness was coming from outside me, rather than from within me. I felt something was being inflicted on me. To begin with, my grief stormed in like a rampaging terrorist high on amphetamines and armed, lawless, violating boundaries, destroying my history, my future and with a hysterical disregard for time and place. I was blindsided, and mutely submitted to the position of hostage without complaint. Like any sensible prisoner, I learnt quickly that to protest would make no difference, and choiceless, I submitted to this saboteur with no prospect at all of release or freedom. I believed for a long time that I would never feel differently. I felt a painful absence and loneliness *all of the time.* Sometimes this was combined with a fear that something awful was about to happen to me or to one of my sons. It was existing, rather than living as I had known it, and although I had love and support from family and friends, nothing made any difference at all. It was the bleakest of times.

I dreaded waking every day because I was back in my life without Andrew, rather than in my dreams where he might appear. Every morning I would count how many seconds and then minutes it was before I remembered he was gone. For a long time I would find myself patting the mattress as I woke, searching for him.

Looking back, I think in the months following his death I regularly experienced brief 'short circuits' with reality, fleetingly, privately, which robbed me of the language to describe where I went. This explanation feels inadequate compared to the phenomena. At the time these episodes began, I was not scared. I felt as if I had somehow left myself and gone elsewhere. Maybe this was because my reality had gone – he had gone – so what was left to fear?

And then, a week or so after his death, I took up a strange, secretive, early-morning (and usually nightly) routine. I would wake up before my sons, one of whom, the seven-year-old, had installed himself in Andrew's side of the bed. In the corridor next to our bedroom were fitted wardrobes. The left side was where Andrew kept his suits and some jackets. For a month or so, once, or more often twice a day, I would get into this wardrobe and sit in the darkness. There I would inhale the smell of his suits for ten or fifteen minutes at a time. If I did not do it, I felt wrong, deprived, I imagine like a diabetic who has not taken their insulin. At night, once the children were in their beds, I would climb in, at first listening out for one of them to come down a flight of stairs to find me, and then ten minutes or so later, relaxing into the experience of being there, in a place that was only his. However, the strangest and most important element of this to me – at the time – was that in the middle of the suits were two crumpled, white cotton shirts that had been put back, without being laundered, in the wardrobe, I presumed by Andrew, deliberately, for me. He was communicating with me.

Andrew was highly organised and his shirts had gone to the laundry every two weeks. They returned, as he specified, folded, and with a minimal but important dose of starch on the collar, and sheathed in cellophane. They were stored in piles on shelves that lined the wardrobe to the right of the deeper hanging space. He would wear one a day until the whole lot was sent off again to the laundry and the other ten or twelve came back.

I had been fascinated by this precise arrangement when we first got together, a sort of professionalisation of his clothes. I liked, admired and envied his precision. I also felt he knew his way around life, in a way that I, six years younger, did not. There was a rhythm and routine to his daily habit. He stuck to things, loyally, the same type of soap, toothpaste, medicines, shirtmaker, sock. He bought in bulk in Boots or John Bell & Croyden, six tubes of aqueous cream or Beconase at a time and ordered his shirts three at a time. Was he frightened he might run out? There was something of that. But unlike me, constantly looking for something new and better to try, wasting money on a face cream that could only disappoint, Andrew, it felt to me, had done his research in life carefully and methodically, and knew what was right for him. He liked to know there would be provision and planned accordingly. He semi-joked it was an aspect of his Judaism, an intergenerational transmission, a trait of anxiety. What I observed was that he was at one with his needs, comfortable with his body, sure-footed. He wasn't wasteful, but had developed careful and appreciative routines for himself that made him unreliant. I liked how little he needed me, and how he didn't expect me to look after him, though for me it was pleasurable to do so, as he was so appreciative. He couldn't boil an egg but could make toast and tea, and iron.

Unlike me, he did not throw clothing on the floor at night when getting ready for bed. His jerseys were carefully folded, chest up, sleeves invisible, his trousers went into his trouser press and his ties were rolled into a honeycomb-shaped wooden contraption he had on another shelf. With him arrived a bag full of shoe polishes and rags, the tins of wax not thrown out until they were rubbed down to the edges. Each week I would find him sitting wide-legged on an armchair in our bedroom, buffing carefully away at his black loafers or lace-up shoes, his large biceps tight under a suit sleeve as he prepared his expensive footwear for the business meetings ahead, readying himself for the battle of commerce, wanting to look his best. I found it admirable and touching. A shorn, burnished Roman gladiator, holding up each shiny black shoe, inspecting it minutely.

Yet there they were, next to the suits, two shirts

glowing white in the darkness of the row of grey and black jackets, deadly sober on their mahogany hangers. Both were creased, one also had a small ink stain on the left cuff, and both had definitely been worn. I remember feeling nauseated excitement when I saw them. I believed that this was evidence that he was going to come back, after all, particularly if I followed his instructions, which I was sure would come. I was convinced there was an enormous significance to the presence of these shirts and that he had opened up a channel for communication with me that I must not tell anyone else about. If I did, it might be spoilt in some way or destroyed, and potentially I would lose him completely. So, at the time, during those morning immersions in the wardrobe, I believed a takeover of me by Andrew was under way. He had not left me after all, and he might be back.

I could find no other way of explaining why he had left the shirts there. It was inconceivable that he had not left them there on purpose. I believed this was vital signposting, left for me, in anticipation that I would find the shirts and wait for the next missive. I absolutely *did not know* it was completely mad and impossible that this was the case, not least as there were any number of ordinary rational explanations as to how the shirts had ended up there, all of which had nothing to do with Andrew.

But oh, those shirts. I would gently shake one of them off the hanger from my position below it and sniff deeply. I rotated the two of them strictly so as to not run out of the smell in either of them. I would then strip off my pyjama top to put the shirt on and pull the collar up so it touched the base of my skull, rubbing my head on it. Did I lick them? Yes, I think I might have done on occasion. I know I often kissed the fabric, rubbed it on my face. On his collar was his aftershave, on the armpits, his safe clean scent, and on the cuffs more of it, a little greying on one of them, the dark patch from his Lamy ballpoint on the other. The wardrobe door had to be shut to stop his smell escaping while I sat inside. If it was left open I shut it immediately. The smell would be wasted! Sometimes I would sit there wordless, thoughtless; sometimes I found myself crying. However, I felt grateful for this substitute that was nothing like the real thing and yet for short bursts of time calmed the raging confusion in my head about where he had gone. When I heard stirring or had to get my sons up, I would get out, checking that neither of them might see my exit had they happened to come down from the floor where they slept. Then, carefully, I put the shirts back in situ, looking like a normal person, standing busily outside the wardrobe, just straightening the contents up, checking everything was neat and tidy, as he used to do.

How long did this continue? I can't recall.

I did not, at the time, see the relationship I had with the two shirts as at all odd or abnormal. On the contrary, I saw it as a preservation of him, a duty, a way of keeping him with me. It was a critical part of the day for a while. My more rational self said if I could not have his body, I would at least have his cells, his DNA from these shirts, on me. This was the explanation I was prepared to offer had someone found me with his shirt on. My private unconscious understanding was different, a game of divination was in play and the truth is that at that early stage I did believe we might be led back to each other. Would it be me to him, him to me? Impossible to say.

This sort of thing (what else can I call it?) went on for around 28 months, in many different ways, less ritualised later on than the business with the shirts, and gradually easing in length and severity. I now see the experiences as terrible, urgent reckonings with the fact he was dead, and I would never see him again.

Once I was motionless in a chair for several hours, a quadriplegic seizure of an ordinarily functioning body. I could not move, and sat staring out of the window onto our garden. Once I had to stop driving as I was on the wrong side of the road, but could not remember which was the right side. I got to the side and half-parked the car on the pavement, annoying a woman with a pram, who glared at me. I did not dare try to straighten the car as I could not think how the key turned in the ignition. I just sat there and waited until it passed, not even knowing that this was what I was doing. Who knew that grief could interfere with your motor skills, quite literally in this case?

Another time, more seriously, and again in the car, I could not remember which pedal was the accelerator and which the brake. At that moment I was at the top of the steep hill that flies you down into the valley before our village. It was as if I had no mind in those seconds and the realisation of his gone-ness was vastly more consuming than the road hurtling downwards and the tons of metal around me. I remember looking at the sharp green blur of the late-May afternoon and feeling a calm but total dislocation. Our house, which we had spent a year of our weekends enjoyably looking for, was a mile or so behind me. What did I think in that moment? That it was beautiful and that we had loved that house, and that place, but that he was gone, so nothing mattered any more, and neither did I.

I will say that the children weren't in the back that day.

With hindsight, I think something like this happened nearly every day, for several hundreds of days after his death; a feeling of abrupt shock, a wallop in my face, a winding in my solar plexus. Imagine it as if someone grabbed the back of your collar and pulled you back hard. Then ran away. I was stopped sharply in my tracks. Speechless. Sometimes a second, sometimes longer.

Gradually, these episodes began to diminish. Bluntly, and from a cognitive perspective, I got used to it – it became a familiar feeling; I began to *know*, without thinking, that he was gone, in the same way you know that your hand is attached to your wrist or that water comes out of the tap when you turn it on. I began to slowly believe, unconsciously, on a different plane to the conscious mind, that he was never ever coming back.

A friend asked me a few months ago when I disclosed all of this, what I thought *he* would have thought. *About the shirts?* And without thinking at all I said: *He would*

have been pleased, he would have been very happy I
was so devastated... That I sat in his wardrobe loving
his bloody shirts. (The friend – and I – laughed.)

At the time I told no one.

3

News

This is what happened.

My work was coming to an end, that day – an ordinary wintry Thursday afternoon. The week before Christmas, and I had one more patient to see, the last of the year. The children had broken up, and the days before the 25th were going to be full but enjoyable, seeing friends for drinks, tidying the house, cooking, preparing things, buying presents and so forth. The newness of being together was still thrilling to us. We had a new home together, we could make plans together. We were shiny with excitement, and in charge.

That night we had arranged to have supper with a couple, Stewart and Camilla, to whom we were both close. I had realised at five that I had still not agreed with Camilla where we were going to meet for supper, which I had promised to do.

My patient was late and I looked briefly at my phone, wanting to reply to Camilla, who was asking for a plan for time and place. Instead, a text arrived from Andrew as I looked. *Results back, pls meet me at GP.* I was sitting in my chair, and had to think what he meant.

What results? It was this insignificant. It meant nothing, absolutely nothing. I racked my memory for anything he had said.

Some explanation is needed. He was very sporty; I am not. I understood it from the moment I first saw him walking down the street to meet me, and later, in the way he moved around our house. He jogged up and down the stairs, carefully supported his core when he bent his spine, stretched, lifted weights (and anything else) correctly and possessed a sort of bodily flair I have never had. We also talked about our bodies' failings and deficits in very different ways. I basically hoped and still hope that nothing will go wrong with my body. We understood our bodies would require more attention as we aged and as they ceased perhaps to be our obedient slaves and gofers. He understood this perfectly and was attentive and never in denial. He knew that it was already beginning in quiet ways: a slipped disc here, a hernia there – he was 51, after all. He sometimes talked about how happy he would be in his seventies, not 'giving up', as he put it, which he disapproved of, but accepting the changes wrought by age as they came along, and adapting to them. Perhaps only the truly athletic see things in these terms. His standards were much higher than mine, which seemed superficial and amateurish in comparison. I have only ever thought about my physical self and its possibilities in prosaic ways, wishing or hoping I won't get fat, or wondering if there is any way of diminishing wrinkles, but knowing there is not.

His relationship with his body was very different; realistic, harmonious, knowledgeable and demanding. There was nothing adversarial or disappointed about it; he did not lament its past. He thought critically about performance and ability. He had been a county athlete as a boy, a serious footballer, tennis player and skier. He had turned down a golf scholarship, but become a scratch golfer in adulthood. I had never been on a green in my life. His serious golf playing was curtailed by me in a way, but not unhappily, and he would come to the gym with me, so we could spend more time together. But I watched him as he did weights or used a running machine, and there was something different from other people in the way he carried out a set of lifts or ran for twenty minutes. He regarded his body as an ally and helpmeet.

We walked at weekends, marking up steps, more for my benefit and satisfaction than his, and crossing the park opposite our house during the week, always talking, holding hands, speeding up, slowing down. I was envious of the way his own body maintained itself, remaining muscled and taut. He sometimes said something hurt but never made a fuss, and took himself off for an ultrasound or physio, seemingly very alive to the legacy of all the sport he had done. I thought about my physical self differently, carelessly, with crossed fingers, whereas he was respectful and vigilant, having cared for this hardy and yet sensitive machine all his life. He understood that in order to have a body that served you well, you had to take notice of what it felt like and attend to problems.

We were both about to see that all this attention and care could be suddenly and violently sabotaged by an illness that does not reward the careful or the diligent.

Rolling through our conversations in my mind in those minutes, I did remember a sore knee – or was it his hip? – that he had meant to get his GP Dr Siddiqui, or Wasi, as he called him, to look at, but didn't know if he had or not. The text must have related to the knee, the hip or perhaps something in his shoulder, where he had a perennial issue. *Ah that was it. His shoulder. It must be one of those things*, I thought in those seconds, *it must be...*

A couple of minutes passed and still the patient had not arrived. But another text did. In capitals.

PLEASE GET HERE.

In that next minute my mind would still not go there, and with increasing fervour I told myself he must have taken a cancellation that morning, it was for a knee scan, he'd changed an appointment with Wasi last week... *Yes, he had come with me to a school thing for one of the children...* I was suddenly absolutely clear. I felt my shoulders spread, my heart slow, and I put the phone to the side of my chair. *OK, OK, calm down.*

Within about three minutes, I suddenly realised that there *was* something, something I had chosen to forget, and I felt my stomach begin to simmer.

Then the bell rang and there was the patient, nine minutes late, which meant I had 41 minutes to try and listen to her against the sound of my own heart beating and the feeling of moisture gathering on my scalp and under my arms. At 5.52pm I ran, without a coat, without saying anything to the children or hassling anyone to do their viola practice, their holiday maths, just a shout to our housekeeper, Shards, that I would be back and to stick them on Minecraft if they wanted. *I'm just popping out, Shards, hold the fort, please! Thank you.* Over the Marylebone Road, a 400-metre stretch, in my flat thin-soled pumps, which hit the pavement hard every half-second, jarring my knees; my fitted trousers and shirt stopping me from charging as I wanted to. I heard my panting and a horn and realised I had not waited for the traffic lights to change at the top of Harley Street. Then there I was, running into a lift, into the now emptying clinic, shown into an overheated room on the top floor of the building above a dark Regent's Park. A thin blonde Polish receptionist looked at the doctor behind his desk and asked if that would be all.

Thank you, Magda, yes. Could you be a darling and ring Mrs P and tell her I am going to be a little delayed? The door closed behind me.

Andrew's back was in front of me, in the corduroy jacket he had left the house in that morning. He barely looked at me as I came in, but sat, his legs apart, elbows on the doctor's desk, his hands as if in prayer, head down. But it was not Wasi who broke the news to us that evening. He had left for Mumbai that morning for the Christmas break with his parents. I had never seen the man on the other side of the desk before in my life.

With a brief smile he bowed his head as I was shown

in, and holding out his soft hand, said, like an actor, *I am so very, very glad you're here, Juliet. May I call you Juliet?* A thespian's smile, and a hand over the one already in his palm.

Then he sat down behind the desk, his fingers spread wide and theatrically over the shiny walnut.

There is bad news, regrettably. Andrew, you have cancer, but we don't, I am afraid, know where yet, nor how serious.

Words that sounded, simply, improbable. Hackneyed, certainly, even jokey – I would do impressions of him later for Andrew, during the brief foolish period when we thought we had been lucky. All this was to come, but I think I knew then how mortally serious this might be for him, and for me. Andrew sat, his leg crossed high over his knee, his elbows now back.

OK, help me understand here.

He drew himself up, his head straight on his broad shoulders, and put both hands, palms down, noisily on the desk. An aggressive order to this idiot doctor, who I had a vague recollection of Andrew mentioning as someone who had been put into 'locum' retirement as he was too old to be in general practice.

Ah.

The doctor, smarmy, facetious, his hands prayer-like beneath his chin was enjoying this.

Andrew, Andrew, Andrew. We don't know much yet. We know, as your good GP Dr Siddiqui had requested your blood tests be processed immediately, that the teeny weeny lump in your neck that he examined yesterday is a cancerous – he hesitated for greater effect – *tumour.* He turned his hands upwards, apparently helpless, to the ceiling. *It must, simply, must have come from some-where else. This much we do know. It is what we call a secondary. So, old chap, we're going on a cancer hunt.*

He paused, looked at me and smiled patronisingly.

I'm so sorry. Such really rotten luck. Really terrific-ally bad luck. He grimaced and tilted his head to one side. *Now, we've managed to make an appointment with a chest man, don't know him myself but honestly, you're lucky, given the timing and so forth. Christmas etcetera! He can see you now, so I suggest you rather hot-foot it over to him, and he can advise you in more detail of what happens next. Once again, so sorry. Terribly sorry.*

We ran, holding hands, me without a coat, the cold beginning to close down tight on the evening. We hurtled through Devonshire Place, both of us good runners, past building after building, confused by the even and odd numbers. *Here, here*, we slowed down as we saw the clinic and, sweating, ran into the quiet reception, where a young woman sat, her coat over her shoulders, her bag on the desk next to her, poised to be taken as soon as she had dispensed us. She immediately directed us up to the fourth floor, via a small wooden lift, accompanied by a tired-looking old porter she clicked her fingers at. The three of us stood in the tiny space, looking down.

The slight, brown-eyed consultant met us at the door. He was younger than both of us and had a fleece under his jacket over his shirt and tie. He had seen his last patient of the day but had agreed to stay to see us.

He welcomed us into his large consulting room. It was rented by the hour and hotel-like in its impersonal corporate style. He smiled kindly.

I'm Doctor Nayam. I'm sorry to meet you under these circumstances. Ahm... I think you may have just been told you've got cancer? He raised his eyebrows and grimaced.

We nodded. *Yes.* Andrew took my hand. *Yes, we have. I have.*

The doctor slightly shook his head, his hands clasped in front of him on the table, but seemed somehow thoughtful and kind. He was about to speak when his mobile flashed, a pretty woman dressed up for a wedding with two small olive-skinned children in silk jackets blinking on the screen.

I'm sorry. That's my wife wanting to know what I'm doing. He smiled, lips closed, a little embarrassed.

We shook our heads, of course he should call her. *Take it, take it, please,* said Andrew.

He texted briefly and turned back to us, placing his phone in a drawer.

Sorry.

It's fine, it's fine. We shook our heads in unison.

I saw my phone light up too, six missed calls now from Camilla.

Look, first of all, I'm sorry, it really isn't appropriate the news is broken in that way. It's really bad, I do apologise. I'm just... We all three nodded, *outrageous, yes, really bad, not appropriate,* and I saw how swiftly we left facts behind and swam fast to something else, something we would start to do a lot.

We all agreed it had not been ideal, but now I know he was apologising for something different. The more we concurred avidly that the last hour of Andrew's life had been badly managed, the more I thought we were all avoiding the fact we had been told something true and terrible.

At some profoundly hidden level, I think, I also knew at that point, on 19th December, at around 7pm, that our future could become an end. This may sound unlikely, but unconsciously, I think I did. We were quite mute at that point, so shocked that the right questions weren't even there. Really, neither of us knew anything at all about cancer; had certainly never known anyone with lung cancer. We sat there, quietly wanting to know, to not know what we wanted to know, but to get back out into the night, and our lives. To not leave too, because who knew what to do with a tumour in the lung?

The consultant was professional and straightforward, and brokered a plan, making calls in front of us to ensure Andrew would be scanned before the long already frightening Christmas closing of the clinics and hospitals began. We left, fifteen minutes or so later, agreeing we would see him the next afternoon, in the same room, to discuss the next steps.

It was very cold as we stepped out, making me gasp. Andrew immediately took his coat off and put it over my shoulders, holding my hand tightly, then pulling me close to him on Portland Place as we walked in speeded-up synchronicity. We did not speak for those first few minutes. He gripped me, one arm around my front, one around my back, and I did the same to him. A frightened three-legged race home.

We were soon back at our house, where Stewart and Camilla awaited us, uninvited and concerned. I had sent only one text to her, as I ran to meet Andrew to say that we might be delayed. Her intuition and experience had told her there was a problem.

OK, what's happening, you guys? She came to the door of our sitting room as we came up the stairs, her American accent direct and insistent.

Their nine-year-old son had survived a brain tumour, diagnosed when he was six. During his illness she had given up work to become the custodian of his life. I had watched in awe as she dedicated herself to him, stopping work for a year, during which time she had tutored him carefully during his frequent stays in hospital, argued furiously on the best course of action with doctors, read up on all the research, contacted consultants in foreign hospitals, ordered changes to his drug regime and demanded resources. She had become an expert on his illness, made a study of it, and considered it forensically from every angle of her son's present and his future.

I saw her face as Andrew told her inside our hallway that he had just been informed he had cancer and felt she was not surprised. The residual expectation of those who have been told, out of nowhere, they or their loved ones have cancer.

By nine the four of us sat, slumped on our sofas,

drinking wine fast, takeaway food forgotten in cartons in front of us. Camilla had begun to plan, to give us strategies: *This is who you will need, this is who you need to ask, for this is how you do this, I am going to do that, this is going to be how you manage it.* Andrew and I listened intently.

As they left an hour later, Stewart touched Andrew's arm. *This is your disease, mate, no one else's, and you must deal with it as you want to.* I nodded encouragingly to Andrew. It was something he repeated to me often. *It's my disease, I'm dealing with it my way.* Several years later, I would say to Stewart that I wished he had never said that to Andrew. He had unwittingly suggested he take ownership of something that he had no purchase on or control of at all.

Did I know, that he had been given a death sentence? Impossible to say, but I do know that from that point on I did not allow myself to entertain the thought, so it remained, half hidden,and half present in a repressed recess of my brain for the next 14 months. Repression is a most useful tool. I will sometimes advise patients to deploy repression for a fear of flying or surgery or some other terror, because there is nothing else to be done. The plane must generally be boarded, the operation generally submitted to. *Stop the thought when it comes and think of something else.* Not very analytic, perhaps, but highly effective.

4

Scotomisation

The blind spot in the retina is called the scotoma. It comes from the Greek word *skotos* (to darken) and means a spot on the visual field in which vision is absent or deficient.

In psychoanalysis, scotomisation is a capacity to not see, to ignore what is visible. In a patient we talk about this blind spot as 'the seeing and not seeing' part of themselves. This characteristic is a defence mechanism, used to reduce anxiety in very difficult or traumatic situations.

From this point onwards, wanting to see something or not see it became an important part of the way we lived. We chose not to see.

An hour or so after Stewart and Camilla left, we got to bed. Andrew somehow, perhaps through shock, was quickly deeply asleep. I, with my blood full of adrenaline and the strong red wine I had continuously sucked down into an empty stomach all evening, was wide awake.

I could not sleep at all that night (unusual for me) because I had remembered the precise moment – erased until then from my conscious memory – that he had taken my hand from my book, pulled my index finger to him and brought it up to his neck, the left side, ten centimetres down from his chin, and laid it there. I replayed it again and again in my mind until light began to leak a grey grouting through the shutters of our bedroom.

It was 22nd November 2013, a month or so before. We were in New York.

Had we known it, this was the day our life and our relationship were about to dramatically change direction. It was a Saturday morning and we were in our hotel, having arrived late the night before. He had work to do and I had gone with him so we could spend a long weekend together. We were high up, on the 40th floor of a hotel he liked. It was completely silent, the carpets and thick glass insulating the room's occupants from the noise of the city. His city, where he had done many successful deals early in his career, a place he had spent a lot of his twenties and thirties commuting to and from London, two decades before I knew him. He'd often insist I wouldn't have liked him had I met him back then; that I would have found him brash and aggressive. But I was impressed by how well he knew the streets, identifying every building I asked about, knowing precisely where he wanted to go, and eat, showing me museums and galleries. The pre-dawn darkness of a winter's morning. Silence other than the *Today* programme from the iPlayer app which was always playing on his phone wherever he woke up. The 50th anniversary of Kennedy's shooting, bombing in Iraq by Sunni groups, a delay to Obamacare. Why do I remember any of this?

Love?

Yes? I was immersed in my book.

Love.

He pulled my hand over his bare chest up to his neck. The sheet exposed me and I shivered in the air-con breeze, pulling it back up.

Feel this.

I can't feel anything. I'm cold.

Yes, you can. Here. He pushed insistently between the tendons below his ear. *Here.*

An Iran nuclear deal appears imminent, things are looking up in Geneva, John Humphrys was saying. My attention goes.

Sweetie, I'm sorry but I can't feel anything. It feels normal. One hundred per cent.

Here.

Oh, OK, there. Hmm.

What? Do you feel it?

I let him press my fingers more forcefully down into the muscle. There was something. But so small it bounced off my fingertips as soon I felt it.

OK. Yes. I do. Something. But it's miniature. Tiny. I think it's your glands. I always have lumps and odd things there. Feel my neck, feel it. I pulled his hand to my neck then onto my chest and smiled at him. *Feel this.* He wasn't smiling.

I turned onto my side and pulled the sheet over my shoulder, looking up at him, patting the mattress for him to lie down and look at me.

Do you think you're feeling a bit stressed by everything? Your life is stressful. Our life is. Your glands are probably fighting off some infection. Don't worry so much. We've just flown here. You're run down. Go and see your Wasi when you go back if you're worried. Didn't you say your knee needed an ultrasound anyway? It's also quarter to six in the morning. Shall we try and get a little sleep?

Hmm.

I looked at him. He was stroking his neck again, insistently. Looking away, at the door.

It doesn't feel right to me.

Love, you're fine. I promise. We had a running joke about how many visits he made to Wasi to get his opinion. *Get the knee and your imaginary tumour checked out then.* I winked, pulled myself up again and opened my book. Did I feel a little cruel saying that? I certainly do seeing it written down now.

Fuck you. He tilted his chin haughtily to me and resumed reading his iPad.

That moment. Then we smiled at each other.

We didn't discuss it again. We each read our books. We slept for several hours, then walked in Central Park ending up for brunch in a restaurant called Winter that he liked on the Upper East Side. It was the last day before it closed for the winter, to be opened again in spring – *and called Spring* – the waiter told us.

As we ate, we admired the huge twiggy structures that sprang up from the middle of each table, and the realistic frost on every glass.

Great idea, he said, *we should come back for spring and see what they do.*

The restaurant would have had four more names before his death, Spring, Summer, Fall, Winter. For some reason I remembered precisely the face of the young manager as he stood next to his beaming coat-check man, proud as Andrew told him what a great concept he had there.

Well done.

So strange what is remembered and what is forgotten. By this point, after we had eaten, the little lump had completely disappeared in my mind.

Then we walked to the Frick Collection, and wandered holding hands around its large rooms. Art was a great pleasure he had taught himself to enjoy. I would see something and lose him, then find him again. That part of the day too I remembered precisely. His way of looking at me, so kindly, his large dark-brown eyes with their black lashes, sooty and long, a contrast with his shaven head. His habit of standing with his hips forward, one hand clasping the opposite elbow, and an index finger on his cheek, studying a painting. The frequent adjustment of his glasses, with his middle finger pushing them back up his straight, narrow nose. The blue swing of his jacket vents, covering his neat figure, the pockets of his cords on his bottom. My ardour for him, in the absence of children, of work, in a foreign city; the prospect of uninterrupted time together; 72 hours to think only about each other. The way he called for me. *Love. Come here. Come and look at this.*

I remember this day too precisely, which is what is so agonising. I have often since wished I could not remember it so well. Not remember what I lost.

Freud used the term *Nachträglichkeit* (afterwardness) to describe the deferred effect of an event on a person. In the moment that it happens, it just happens. Nothing more. The trauma is realised later when the event becomes imbued with meaning and importance. Sometimes this becomes clear in the presence of an analyst, or the person may reach the realisation by themselves. It may relate to a traumatic event, only understood retrospectively, for example when a child reaches a later stage of sexual development. Freud explained it as an appearance from the past which provides an opportunity for the trauma to be worked through in the present. Temporality – time, and timelessness – is important to humans and one of the cornerstones of psychoanalysis. Time can allow the possibility of something from the past, buried, forgotten, not traumatic at the time, to be processed. We may seek and achieve timelessness in drug-induced states, in daydreaming or in sexual or religious ecstasies, for example. And in depression time ceases to be felt; the past cannot be mourned, the future cannot be envisaged, and time seems to be frozen in an everlasting moment, like death itself.

I wanted that instant when he said something was wrong to be forgotten. I wanted the time to be gone. The fact that I promised him it was nothing was now full of terrible significance. It was not a fact; it was a fantasy on my part, and on his. I think that he absolutely knew that something devastating was drawing his finger to his neck. Yet at that moment, for me it was meaningless. For many, these sorts of moments will remain a sunken memory for ever, for they have no consequences.

Our will, both mine and his, that it was nothing would be forcefully crushed, 27 days from that brilliant Manhattan Saturday morning, when the little bump's true nature was revealed to him, by Wasi's skilled finger-tips. Andrew had indeed taken a cancellation, for his knee, and at the end of the consultation asked the doctor to feel the tiny pea on his throat. Wasi had squeezed the appointment in at lunchtime before catching the train from Paddington to meet his family at the airport, and sent him directly for blood tests, a biopsy and scans. He wrote Andrew an email the next day to apologise for having had to go, but his wife and children were waiting for him at the airport. He hoped he had left us in good hands and would be back soon. Hence the locum. In the email he explained how as soon as Andrew asked him to examine the bump, *it felt springy, full, I just knew, really I am so sorry. I knew there and then.* All the tests he had ordered immediately confirmed his intuition.

The touch of Andrew's own finger knew it already though. Apparently this is not uncommon. The finger finds its way to something protruding, that should not be there, rising up from the body, shaping the skin differently.

Six months later, the scorching radiotherapy over, and the chemotherapy somehow survived Superman-like, Andrew would tell of this moment in New York.

The moment came back as his keen physical sense that he, the man who knew his body so well, discerned there was something wrong, and thank God, he had found the little lump in time. Thank God for a lifetime of taking care. Partial truths became a way of life. It was true, he had found it, but that was really all that was true. Timing is everything. And nothing.

5

An Explanation

In the coming pages I want to describe how I came to psychoanalysis, although many of its ideas have developed into what is more ordinarily called psychotherapy. Psychoanalysis is a treatment, a practice, a science, an art to some, but most importantly a theory of the mind and how it works. There are many differences between psychoanalysis and psychotherapy still under debate but this is not the subject of this book.

People outside are puzzled by the conventions of psychoanalysis; the use of the couch, a patient lying down, the silent analyst sitting unseen behind them, the five-times-a-week (*really?*) frequency of sessions. Its extraordinary nature is a mystery to those wanting to know more but baffled by a series of strange and unlikely rules. The careful framework and boundaries are very important, but it is not even the free association (the patient saying whatever comes to mind before the clinician expertly interprets what might be going on in their unconscious) that really matters.

The untold and immense value of psychoanalysis is

for the patient to gain knowledge of themselves. Simply, someone understands better how all the different parts of their person work. Life is less frightening, less unpredictable, difficult feelings become more tolerable. The point is to make life more bearable, and richer for it.

This comes from the shared unconscious mind of the analyst and the patient working together to explore its depths over years. It is not a treatment for everyone. Not everyone needs it and certainly many would not want it. However, for those who can bear it, and find the time and money to pay for it, the benefits can last a lifetime. In this book, I am trying to suggest how we react unconsciously to a traumatic and unexpected death, and so I need explain why I started to think this way.

I had first come across Freud's paper 'Mourning and Melancholia' when I began, with a hesitant yet persistent interest in psychoanalysis, on a foundation course at the Tavistock and Portman NHS Trust in Hampstead. It was 2003 and I was working in the civil service, but treading water. One afternoon a week, I was allowed what the Cabinet Office called 'a day release' to attend the course at 'the Tavi', which would precede a Masters in Organisational Consultancy. I had realised during my short time working in government that I was not cut out for the work. I lacked the craftiness and subtlety needed to prosper as a civil servant and I was confused by the jargon and acronyms, as well as somewhat bored. I was, however, very interested in what went on in the office. I kept thinking that there must be some way to explain people's behaviour and why they did what they did at work. The Cabinet Office was the perfect place to observe this, if only I could find a way of interpreting it.

I would rush on the Tube from Westminster to Swiss Cottage to spend a Tuesday afternoon in the tatty 70s block at the bottom of Fitzjohn's Avenue. A large and arresting bronze statue of Freud, his legs apart, his fist resting impatiently on his knee, is positioned imposingly at the junction with Belsize Avenue, hinting at what kind of thing might be going on inside. The building itself is full of wilting African violets, triffid-like ferns and brown carpet tiles, and I was hooked by the end of my first seminar, on my first day there.

This idea that there was an unconscious axis to life, which could explain your thoughts and feelings, your wishes and those of others through dreams, slips of the tongue (parapraxes) and a simple and yet complex feeling between you and this mysterious person called a psychoanalyst was both exciting and a relief to me. It was like arriving in a foreign country but feeling I might easily learn the language. I felt at home. Someone, a psychoanalyst, could interpret for you what was going on inside, and you could learn to do it too – *learn to symbolise your internal landscape*, as the nice tutor with wispy hair, large teak beads and a loose brown jumper and green skirt said.

Sixteen years later, by profession I am a psychoanalytic psychotherapist. I first saw patients in a primary-care-trust-funded psychotherapy unit in Kentish Town. Now I have a private practice, seeing patients in my consulting room in North London. My patients come to see me once, twice or sometimes several times a week for 50-minute sessions. They sit opposite me on a chair or lie on a couch with me behind them.

They talk, I listen.

At my sons' school, or at a party, when people find out what I do, they will sometimes ask me who comes to see me, or if I deal with anything special. I generally say that I work with anyone, just like me, or them, usually when a relationship, actual or felt, has ended in some way, recently or in the past. The loss is often unacknowledged, and the reason for the person's distress, anxiety or depression is hazy, or indeed absent. I say I am there to make interpretations. Those who look or ask for the name of someone like me do so because something is bothering them, upsetting them, or very much disturbing them. (By this stage the casual acquaintance asking is either even more curious or has lost interest completely.)

If I feel it is right to go on I say the following.

My job is to try to tell the patient what they don't know – not what they do already. Their only job is to free associate, just to see what comes to their mind, and try to express it. I have to try and create the conditions for them to be able to want to speak, or show me how it feels to be them.

An important aspect of the work is to make interpretations. It can only happen with trust and time, and as the relationship develops between my patient and me.

Freud, working as a general physician in Vienna more than 150 years ago, began to develop the set of ideas that gave rise to psychoanalysis and almost all the many different forms of psychotherapy that exist today. He realised, by trial and error (and an almost total conviction of the powers of hypnotherapy to begin with) that there was a role for a 'talking cure' – a conversation between a specially trained doctor and a patient in which the doctor might be able to reveal what was happening unconsciously in the patient's mind, by careful listening and interpretations. It could be said that everything we today call a 'therapy' derived from his original insights into the mind. Both psychotherapy and psychoanalysis are a way of looking at the human being in developmental terms, but as an individual, unique in the context in which they have lived their life.

My mind needs to be cleared if possible, at the beginning of every one of the 20 to 25 sessions I do a week, ready to engage with what is going on in the room between the patient and me in that moment. What do I feel when the patient sits or lies down? Children know this feeling instinctively, and often have strong, visceral reactions that they are not afraid to voice. However, as we grow up this capacity is trained out of us largely to avoid hurting other people's feelings. *Mum, that man over there looks really strange and I know he wants to murder people. No,* you reply in a reassuring voice, but amused, *he doesn't, love, he's just frowning about how long it is taking him to queue with his shopping trolley.* A small face looks up at you, doubtful.

We learn that we cannot always say what we really feel early on, sometimes for good reasons, and sometimes, with disastrous and lifelong consequences.

Psychoanalysis shares this with flying: the patient, like the passenger, sits back and lets the analyst/pilot do their job. The person who has bought the ticket has almost always chosen the destination and no one can be forced onto a flight. However, especially for very nervous flyers, boarding feels impossible. On most flights, there is always at least a little turbulence, and on many, for even those wealthy passengers in first class, some bodily discomfort. The odd reroute happens, some engine trouble may occur, horrendous weather conditions can arise, but it is extremely rare that planes crash. The pilot, like the analyst, is mapping the terrain below at all times. Gradually, the passenger, perhaps growing interested and familiar with what lies beneath will come to see it themselves, with its challenging impasses, and inhospitable places where it is best not to go, but necessary to be aware of. You never know in life where you will end up, or how you will get there.

Neither psychoanalysis nor psychotherapy aims to cure, nor simply make life 'better' for the patient but rather encourages them to open up their mind to what is really going on. This is achieved by helping them to gain access to their unconscious, through a relationship which is unlike any other they have in their life. I am not friends with my patients; we do not chat. I just expect them to turn up and I hope be open to my invitation to think together during our 50 minutes. A patient may want to interfere and challenge these unspoken elements of the arrangement, asking me questions about myself, for example. I would generally encourage them to wonder about their curiosity about me and see what it yields. Psychotherapy is a treatment, and the therapist may become, for some patients, the most important person they have ever met. The therapist can become the way in which, finally, a patient begins to understand themselves, to have a sense of themselves as integrated, accepting both the good and the bad. At some point, with careful preparation and planning, maybe after many years, there will be an ending, and patient and therapist may never meet again.

I went back to work with my patients four months after Andrew's death. This capacity to treat patients came back before I really found the capacity to be analysed again myself. That took several years, although I never stopped going to analysis, five times a week, as it is an obligatory part of training for a psychoanalyst. But as patients and therapists know, it is possible to turn up to a session and not be there, to take nothing in. I was back on the couch within 48 hours of Andrew's death, five times a week. I think this was a grave mistake. John Steiner, a contemporary psychoanalyst, describes the 'psychic retreat'; a shut-down position in very unwell patients where little can be thought about, and little explored, such is the fear of annihilation. Yet I felt as if my world had actually been blown up and as if any next step, even on the pavement on the way to school with the children, might trigger a land mine. For the first few months or so after he died, my mind was rigidly stuck in America, in the flat we had stayed in while Andrew prepared for immunotherapy treatment. Every day I found myself as if in close-up, staring at the kitchen counter surfaces and blinds of the apartment there. I became fixated with physical residues of the experience, still able to feel the pull of the fridge handle or hear the noise of the doors to the terrace opening. I was unable to move from the scene of his last weeks. But from those early days after Andrew died, I kept my copy of 'Mourning and Melancholia' very close by, on my desk, like a lucky charm. I believed it had a new relevance for me now, both clinically and personally.

6

Mourning and Melancholia

At the Tavi we were set a paper to read, weekly, to help us understand the central concepts of psychoanalysis, and though I didn't retain much detail, in some way I knew I had begun to understand something about life in a way I never had before. Key to this was the hope of an explanation of depression, a condition that had dogged me intermittently since childhood. I had never understood what depression was, though I had sought help and had had three bouts of therapy by the time I got to the Tavistock.

In a way, the experience of depression has influenced me more than anything else in my life. Perhaps it still does. The confusing, unpredictable way in which it had struck, seemingly at random (or so I thought then) was more complex than anything I had ever known. I think that the wish to understand depression, which led me to the Tavi, which in turn led me to start psychoanalysis, was what ultimately made me want to become a psychoanalyst myself.

Sigmund Freud's work has remained the key influence

on how I think about patients on the couch or chair in my consulting room. I am not a Freud academic but I am fascinated by him. The psychoanalyst, Donald Winnicott, hadn't read all of Freud's work, but said he felt him 'in his bones'. Over five decades of study and clinical practice, Freud's ideas underwent complex redefinition, as part of the continuing development of his own mind. Freud worked on and clarified his ideas until he was satisfied he had established what he believed to be the truth. There are 24 thick volumes of what is known as his *Standard Edition* and I certainly haven't read them all, far from it. Within this huge body of work there are, however, essays, concepts and themes that it is necessary to have read and understood if you want to train to be a psychotherapist using psychoanalytic, psychodynamic or relational concepts.

In the seventh week of that first term, working through some of the key Freudian concepts – Oedipus, Dreams, The Drives, The Ego, The Id, Stages of Psychosexual Development – we were handed out photocopied chapters of 'Mourning and Melancholia' to study and bring back for discussion the next week. The essay is one of a series of five published in Volume XIV, *On the History of the Psycho-Analytic Movement, Papers on Metapsychology and Other Works*.

Freud had noticed the similar but drastically different modes and manifestations of both grief from bereavement (or another type of loss, and it is notable he wrote the essay during the First World War) and depression. Both entailed a feeling of a profound absence, but in a depressive state, there was also self-hate and a belief in and need for masochism.

So, back then, long before marriage and children, my interest was in the depression part of the paper, and for the first time in my life, something made sense to me about my own feelings. This idea that a person would not know what they had lost, but might feel profoundly painful dejection, a lack of hope and interest in the outside world, and an inability to love, coupled with an expectation of punishment, sadly resonated with me. That I understood. I sort of grasped the dysfunction that can set off one part of the ego, against its better judgement. Part of the self judges and considers the other part an object, and a nasty one at that. I knew that feeling. The depressed self has a moral disdain for themselves, thinks they really are *bad*, however much they intellectually know they are not. No rational explanation helps. Even the love of people around the sufferer may not help. Freud saw this as an act of displacement. The self-accusations are really all to do with someone else, 'the someone else' that has done the damage. 'They' are not there to hear them, just as they are lost to the sufferer, because having sustained these injuries, the sufferer is lost to themselves. I felt I had understood, or begun to understand, something momentous.

In a powerful evocation, Freud explains what depression feels like. When the subject (the sufferer) fails to get over the loss of a person (the object) through grief and mourning, they become haunted by this person, this loss. *Thus the shadow of the object fell upon the ego so that the latter could henceforth be criticised by a special mental faculty like an object... a forsaken object.* Depression follows, as the subject is thrown into a kind of darkness, unable to truly be seen by themselves or others. Freud is suggesting that the sufferer can begin to feel persecuted and hated by the lost person. Depression feels like hatred. That made sense to me years ago, but now I know that aspects of grief can feel precisely this way too, except not against the self, but against the deceased – a horrible feeling.

Freud also explains that normal bereavement, i.e. grief and mourning, following a *known* loss, a death of someone very much loved, has its own ghastly trajectory for the sufferer. Even though they understand what has gone, and know from a conscious perspective that generally the pain will lessen with time, unconsciously the sense of loss is as powerful as that which results in depression. He provides a succinct encapsulation of the difference between mourning and depression: *In mourning it is the world which has become poor and empty, in melancholia it is the ego itself.*

So I left the civil service, retrained as a clinician, and before Andrew got ill, I knew something about depression, and also bereavement – or thought I did. I had studied and read a considerable amount and treated patients who had suffered significant bereavements recently or historically. I had a structure in my mind for what death does to those left behind. I had studied the impact of death on the living. What I knew has not changed, in one way. I understood that the death of a loved one could disrupt and derail a life for quite a long time. I did not know, however, how little choice the sufferer has when it comes to grief, and how similar this is to depression. How wildly uncontrollable and sado-masochistic it is. I did not know how dramatic the feelings would be; it was like being held underwater by a force that was impossible to overcome or fight against. Hence the notion of any productive 'working through' – such an important tenet of therapy – in my experience made no sense.

Only much later, once I had come out of my own grief and intense mourning, could I begin to impose a trajectory on the last five years, see progress, moments of improvement, recognition and so forth. In my writing, too, as I reorganised it and reread it, I saw how in the first two years after Andrew died I was going here and there, backwards and forwards, but not really moving. I kept on getting stuck. There were months when I had nothing to write or say. My mind was like a suitcase packed full of dirty clothes after a holiday that I carried everywhere with me, that I could not put down. I was full of Andrew, all the time. I thought about him *hundreds* of times a day; our stair carpet would remind me of how he ran down it, a bottle of French red wine would make me think of him, an entire street was him, a white tulip, a car, a breed of dog, a man's coat getting into a taxi. Bond Street. Lacoste shirts. Anything Jewish. Tony Blair. Any tall building. Winston Churchill. An actor he liked. The Masters Cup. Game Theory. Starbucks hot chocolate. Salad cream. Tottenham Hotspur.

It was exhausting. All progress was halted by his death. I was totally immobilised.

But Freud's idea, his model of what happens to someone when their most loved person dies, has stood the test of time – and the idea is accessible to anyone who wants to think about it. Alongside the symptoms and causes of depression, in 'Mourning and Melancholia' he meticulously charts the miserable journey of the sufferer with gentle yet forensic precision, anticipating and even suggesting how long they might feel that way. Yet there is nothing prescriptive here. One reason for this is that the core of the paper related to Freud's experiences of bereavement and depression. There are no patient vignettes in the paper, unusually, no clinical examples to explain the theory, no Wolfman, no Dora, no Little Hans, his most famous patient case studies. 'Mourning and Melancholia' is a personal and painful read, for grief was a causeway he had already begun to travel personally. In 1915, Freud could not of course have known how much further bereavement he would experience nor the long-term effects. But at this point (and he remains the only person to have conducted a self-analysis), he was still very concerned by his father's death at the age of 80 when he was 40. Death, alongside life, had always preoccupied him and there are many examples in his huge correspondence of how he coped with death and empathised with those who had endured losses themselves.

So I always kept my copy of 'Mourning and Melancholia', from that first year at the Tavi, increasingly blurred in its folds, Magic Marker and pencil scribbles all over it, folded up in my bedside table, which changed over the years, as did the person next to me, as one baby, then another came along. It was something I often went back to, puzzling about why I was feeling low, or over a patient whose baffling hopelessness I felt myself struggling with.

Freud is clear. *Melancholias* (Depressions) *show us the ego divided, fallen apart into two pieces, one which rages against the second. This second piece is the one which has been altered by introjection* (the adoption of someone's ideas and thoughts) *and which contains the lost object. But the piece that behaves so cruelly is not unknown to us either. It comprises the conscience, a critical agency within the ego, which even in normal times takes up a critical attitude towards the ego, though never so relentlessly and so unjustifiably.* A central question he was posing, with great prescience, concerns why some people react 'normally' to a painful loss, while others succumb to a depressive state. He notes that unlike 'healthy mourning', which mainly takes place consciously, 'pathological mourning' processes itself unconsciously. Regarding conscious mourning, Freud talks of his own 'polar night', in which he was waiting for the sun to rise. In a polar night there is a sense of time-limitation, of confidence that the sun will rise eventually. The polar night here refers perhaps to his father's death.

In my grief for Andrew, the world felt like a snow-dense prairie, where sky and horizon cannot be differentiated in deep winter. I could not envisage that the snow would melt away, at some point, when spring came. I had been in this position with patients, watching them lost in grief for a loved one. I believed they would recover at some point. It would just take time. *It never occurs to us to regard mourning* (bereavement) *as a pathological condition and refer it to medical treatment. We rely on it being overcome after a certain lapse of time and we look upon any interference with it as useless or even harmful.(Freud, 1917)*

But when it came to me newly in grief – and this seems to me to be another similarity with depression – I could not believe that that greenness, movement and definition between night and day would ever return. It felt totally impossible, beyond elusive. I never hated myself, or felt at fault as I had done when depression struck many years before, but I experienced a tremendous and oppressive darkness around me, removing me from others, leaving me alone. Freud realises that in depression this dead and hopeless landscape is both an internal and an external one. The sufferer is not just alone, but persecuted by a powerful internal saboteur, who tells them that they are bad, worthless, and worse.

Not much else can actively help with grief, he concludes, other than letting the person be – certainly not the psychoanalysis that he prescribes for depression. What is lost is known, and will gradually, in a different way, make its way back.

Grief must be, cannot but be, allowed to luxuriate, settle in and stay as long as it pleases. I am struck by the contrast between this and the swift and efficient passage of a deadly disease through a man's body. Is this to ensure that the sufferer feels as close to death as it is possible for a living person to feel? After several years, one enters a state of sorrowful mourning – rather than being stuck in a desolate mute state of grief – which means that the possibility of expression is returning; expression of love and anger for what or who has been lost, but also renewed expression of love and longing for life and relationships.

But until that point comes, the person living with grief is, every second, every minute, and every hour vitally, and vividly aware of who is lost.

7

The Room Next Door

The Room Next Door, Andrew said, the morning after the day he had gone to get an ultrasound on his knee and was told instead he had lung cancer. 20th December. He had, as usual, woken early and was sitting up in bed, his iPad on his lap, the *Financial Times, Guardian,* and *Times* read cover to cover. I lay feeling bruised, mangled, next to him. I had not slept at all. That first morning I threaded my calves through his legs and laid my head on his chest, wondering what on earth we would do. He put his hand on my forehead, as if checking my temperature, while my ear was above where I guessed his lung was. I listened to his slow even breathing and heartbeat. I stroked his chest, the skin taut and unblemished, bar the odd mole on his brown skin. I found it incredibly strange from the beginning that there was nothing to see of this uninvited tenant of his body. We kept the shutters of our bedroom closed, as the noise from outside gradually began to leak in from the Marylebone Road, and lay for a long time in total silence. I had no thoughts that became words. Other than I felt we were one person. What was his was also mine. I continued to stroke his chest, his arm, his stomach in an unconscious way. Was I checking for other strange growths under his skin? I asked did he want tea, but he refused it. He didn't ask me if he could make me a cup, not that I was expecting him to, but he always did. Something had already changed.

It's like we're here, and it's normal and the world is still spinning and the bills still need paying and you're going to keep driving the boys to school and seeing patients and I'm going into the office and yet, none of it matters. It's so fucking weird. I feel like I am in a different place. Going to Pret a Manger or to fill the car with petrol is completely different, it's nuts... He rubbed my hair, put his palm over my scalp.

I knew what he meant. For we know that in some way we always await bad news. In the same way we discover, at a certain point in childhood, with shock, that one day we will die. Our finiteness is always known to us unconsciously. This is the notion of the death instinct. We are born knowing we will die. Freud's preoccupation with death emerged early on, even before he began writing down his theories. In his 'Beyond the Pleasure Principle', written in 1920, neatly between 'Mourning and Melancholia' and 'The Ego and The Id', he suggests the death instinct is the opposite of the libidinal energy that drives us to seek out pleasure as human beings. We are relentless about seeking pleasure, often despite negative consequences that we know we risk. *The difference between rats and people is that when a rat gets shocked at one end of a maze, he never goes there again.* (DF Skinner, Harvard Lecture, 1959.) Yet we know there will always be a return to nothingness. Freud suggests that death and pleasure are inextricably linked, because we know at some point all this will come to an end. We're just able to forget it, most of the time. That day, though, we were confronted with it.

I mean. How did this fucking happen? A monologue of lucid disbelief. He was talking out loud to himself but for me to hear. Embarrassingly, I was very hungover, my eyes aching in their sockets and my throat dry. Andrew by contrast was highly alert, brisk, articulate.

I know. I know. It's... oh God, love.

I did not have any words; what could I possibly say? I felt a sudden rapid temperature change throughout my body and shivered. I wanted to move.

I patted his legs under the duvet and went to brush my teeth, leaving the bathroom door open. The monologue continued as I sluiced water again and again around my mouth. He related to the room the steps by which, the evening before, an extremely healthy 51-year-old man had been told he had lung cancer. *I'm a sportsman, a scratch golfer, a non-smoker, a healthy eater, I barely drink, I don't... I don't understand.* He looked straight ahead, scratching the top of his shaven head and then banged the iPad down on the floor beside him. *I just don't get it... I...*

I came back in, pulling my dressing gown around

me, now feeling claustrophobic and moment by moment wakening to the horror of our situation. I wanted to see the children and go down and make breakfast and it to be term time and a normal Friday. But it was 6.15am, and both had been on sleepovers, fortunately, given what they still did not know and we were still only beginning to process. There was no school, and we were going to have to work out what to say, both to them and to his children, fairly soon.

Then I heard him say, *It's like we're in a place next door to normal life. The Room Next Door.*

The Room Next Door.

His phrase. This is where you go when you have a serious illness. Of course, we knew we were not alone – we knew the statistics; everyone does. There are hundreds of thousands of people walking in and out of this room, then back into life, every day. Yet the nature of The Room Next Door means you are alone, in a throng of others who you are with but don't meet. A strange new place where death becomes something real, and possible.

We would have the weekend to get through, followed by a thromboscopy on Christmas Eve.

But I saw from the beginning, from that morning, when we lay together in that bed, as I swallowed ibuprofen and downed a pint of water, that this was his illness, and no one else's. He talked about 'we', as always, but he would tell me over the next 48 hours how he was going to run and manage this disease as his own, as carefully and determinedly as he would run one of his deals. He had a plan. No interference would be allowed.

An hour later we sat in the kitchen, me unable to eat, Andrew making a list while I buttered toast for him. I sat on his lap with my mug of tea as he continued to scribble his notes on what he needed to do in the next few days. I felt needy and desperate for what we had heard the night before to be untrue.

I love you but can you get off and sit on your own chair? I dragged the chair next to him over and shifted onto it. He looked at me and puckered his lips into a kiss. He was coming back up again.

OK. Good. So, here's what I think. Listen hard, as we need to make sure we do this and you understand what I want. He then began, as if he had been thinking this through for several days, to explain the following to me. That it was not to be discussed outside our families. He would be telling his adult children more or less the situation, although editing elements of it; mine would be told using different words, sooner because they lived with us, but when the time was right. His family were to know, as were my parents, brother and two cousins. He agreed to my suggestion that my friends Rachel, Jan and Fiona, in addition to Stewart and Camilla who had been there the night before, should also know. And that was it, to begin with. More for my sake than his, as he told me. *There's no point. I'm going to get through it. No one is to know.*

Of course. And I did understand. No one else was to know. I also knew it was a mistake. It almost always is, because of the complicity that it requires of those who love the sufferer to pretend that everything is going to be all right.

From that morning we began casing the new joint together, The Room Next Door, meaning that death did not need to be mentioned. Only when we lay side by side in bed, when it was black and silent and all the distractions of the day were called off, would he start to talk about how strange, how isolating a feeling it was, exploring quietly with me how he felt, off guard.

Survival, however, he also mentioned often – four or five times daily – beating the bell curve, being unusually strong, fit, getting the right doctors. They were strange first days and weeks in this new world of serious but invisible, symptomless illness. Christmas, an odd day but just as we had planned it. The photos show us smiling with all my family raising our glasses to the camera. A picture of contentment. No indication of anything. Then the New Year came, term started, and we stuck to our plans, changed nothing. He, as if it were a new project, scheduled the radiotherapy in the early mornings to fit around his work, and the chemotherapy was planned in at two-week intervals to begin at the end of January. He added the treatment to the rest of his life, and so did I.

Yet I think now we were both continuously completely shocked at that stage, and actually, this never changed, despite the times when, as people with cancer often report, you completely forget for an hour or maybe more that you have the disease. The Room Next Door became an unspoken understanding between us – where everything else stopped mattering. This we did speak about, or we understood somehow how to go in there together. We both knew that this place was one where nothing existed – not us, the children, work, relationships, parents, relatives, sex, friends, houses, holidays, jobs, piano practice, terrorist attacks, money, politics, books, maths prep, food, restaurants, films, window boxes, too much wine, not enough water, salad again, roast chicken or lamb, a 3.15 or 5.45 showing, filling a car with petrol, – *nothing, because it will all be going.* Nothing was left once we were in that room. It is hard to describe what it felt like but it became a way in which we managed our terror. The influential psychoanalyst, Wilfred Bion, talks about the 'nameless dread' (1961) of the infant, surrounded by threats he does not yet understand, and his overwhelming fear of his mother leaving him. I think this is what we both felt. There was comfort in knowing we had each other, but at the same time the constant threat of being split up. Now it seems extraordinary to me that we did not discuss his possible death, but at the time it did not.

Once, late one night, at the end of January, after five weeks of pretending that everything was normal and not telling anyone that my partner had lung cancer, I started to cry and couldn't stop. It was late, we had been out to supper, I had had a few glasses of wine – not least because we no longer kept alcohol at home – and the children were asleep upstairs. I sat on the loo and wept, hiccupping with the tears. *It is absolutely fucking impossible, what he is asking of us, of me. No*

one must know. I live in a prison of fucking untruth.
I felt unable to stop the gush of rage, misery and guilt.
I had become sick of it all that day. In particular, at
the school gate, where at drop-off and pick-up I would
listen to mothers telling me how anxious they were
about the tests our eleven-year-old sons were about to
sit, or how hard it was getting two children to different
tennis clubs when the nanny didn't drive. That afternoon as I waited for the boys, a woman told me she was
seeking psychotherapy to help her manage her concern
and not adversely affect her son's chances of getting into
St Paul's, while another told me *sotto voce* she was on
antidepressants as she was so stressed by the refurbish-
ment of their house in Primrose Hill. Hot with rage, I
had driven the boys home and gone back to work to see
three patients before meeting Andrew for supper with
a couple we didn't know well and who wanted to talk
about politics. It had all been too much.

I had gone into the bathroom after him to wash and
brush my teeth. And started to cry loudly. He had taken
a shower and was in bed, reading. I knew he could hear
me and I knew it would have upset him to hear me.
Eventually, I got up and walked into the bedroom. He
turned out the light as I lay down next to him and took
my hand.

What's wrong? His voice was clear and kind but
hopeless.

I can't say.

You can. You definitely can.

I could not stop myself. Nor the tears.

I'm bloody terrified. That you are going to die and I don't want to have to go through that. It sounds pathetic and all about me and I am so sorry to say it because I know it can't help you but part of me doesn't want to be alive if you're not. I can't bear it. I just can't.

My words sounded almost unbelievable even to me. His thick torso and legs had clamped themselves around me. His breath sweet, his eyes dark and shiny in the dim light from the hallway, left on should one of the children wake in the night and need us. He could not say anything to me then, but held my hand and placed it on his chest.

It's OK, it will be all right. I felt his disappointment.

There was nothing I could say, no way of responding to this obvious denial. We sometimes choose not to see what we know will hurt us.

I felt I had broken the pact. I did not do so again. I could not tell him everything that was going on, as as I used to do. Before, he had known the details of all my thoughts, of my body, of everything. He loved to know. Had to know. Now he could not hear it. He would not be able to bear it. From then on I took it to the analyst and gave it to him. Did it make things easier? Who knows.

Secrecy from the perspective of psychoanalysis always leads to problems for the patient and impasses in the consulting room. Lies. I once heard from a colleague about a consultation with a patient who told him within minutes that he had five children and was about to have a sixth – in effect three families, one wife, two lovers; three mothers. The second knew of the existence of the first woman. The third knew of the second. The first woman was about to discover the existence of the third one. He didn't want my colleague to help him understand his giant web of lies, but rather to help him think of a strategy to cushion the blow. They agreed to an appointment the next week but my colleague felt uneasy as the man merrily left his consulting room, then quite upset that night when he went to bed. The next morning his supervisor carefully listened to his notes of the session and asked him how he felt. He said he had been feeling quite disoriented and strange since the evening before, but couldn't work out why. The supervisor matter-of-factly explained that it was not possible to work with pathological liars and to cancel the next meeting. The patient that wasn't to be had no idea of the consequences for anyone, let alone the five children spawned with the three women. Had my colleague been seduced in the session into thinking he could change him? He was about to become the fourth woman, his gender irrelevant. A lesson learnt.

But a non-pathological liar doesn't believe the lie (that for some reason they tell) and knows that where possible being honest is best. Andrew and I were non-pathological liars. However, the denial that began with Andrew's wish not to tell anyone he had a serious cancer was contagious, compulsive and became increasingly pathological between us. It would lead to terrible damage that could have been avoided. The more coherent and collusive we became, the more his variation of lung cancer (that has still killed everyone whose lungs it has nested in) became something we had under control and could conquer. He didn't conform to the normal statistics, he was superhuman and he and I would have 30 years of life left together. Even if they couldn't get rid of it we would have plenty of time to wait for a new drug that would. We never questioned the future we had planned on, ever.

8

Fuzzy Science

Camilla, there the night of the diagnosis, had rung me the day after and told me we needed a nutritionist, that the evidence showed this could make a big difference and that she had the number of the best one – a gentle and committed practitioner who was on top of the research.

I should see her urgently.

Andrew and I lived, I believe, without much concealment or division between us. Until he became ill and said that no one outside our small tight group must know he had cancer. This was one of the first changes, a fine-mesh barrier that he put up the night we found out. Andrew respected Camilla and said he would be happy for me to see the nutritionist, although he did not wish to meet her.

Fine, you see her. Whatever you need to do. Let's get her in. Do it when I'm at work. I'll do what you say...

The nutritionist came to the house one dark afternoon in late January, just before the radiotherapy was due to start. She was quiet, serious and had taken the train up from Somerset. There had been a lot of communication about the need to get a particular train because of the cost of the day return, although I had said I was happy to pay her fare. She told me she had twins who had never eaten dairy nor had a vaccination.

She was slight and eager, determined to help, although making no promises. She refused tea and brought her own glass bottle of water with her. She sat poised with a large foolscap pad and asked me what I knew about his illness, but I realised I couldn't answer many of her questions and saw her look at me with slightly closed eyes. She wondered whether I could email her some communications from the consultant; sometimes they could be a bit difficult emailing someone like her direct. Nutrition, she said, was beginning to be recognised as important by conventional medicine but sadly, they were not there yet.

She asked to see our fridge next and earnestly peered into its loaded shelves. I saw her clench her jaw as she looked at the packs of Cheddar, Brie, Petits Filous, a joint of lamb and pints of non-organic milk next to a box of macaroons and a family pack of Dairy Milk that Andrew must have bought. He had a very sweet tooth. Closing it gently behind her, she commented that it was absolutely essential that Andrew stop eating any non-organic food immediately as *the metals and toxins might worsen the cancer.* She looked at me and gave an apologetic but worried smile. *I mean, really all of that* – she gestured at our fridge – *I wouldn't let him near it.*

Meat was a bad idea, as it was *hard to digest.* Fish

was a possibility, but not salmon. Or cod. Or bream and definitely not tuna *which was well known as a poison, actually.* What other fish were there? I wondered vaguely as she sat now scribbling on sides of A4 what fresh food was good for him. He should give up tea and coffee, and the water we all drank should be filtered, not from a plastic bottle and most certainly not from a tap. At this point she suggested she should also look inside the cupboards and winced as she saw the tins of tomatoes, baked beans and sweetcorn, Jaffa Cakes, Weetabix and packets of dried pasta, couscous and rice. The problem, she said gently, was that carbohydrates were really not helpful to the body, already under digestive strain with chemotherapy, and, she added after a pause, she really wouldn't recommend he ate any grains or wheat for at least the next year. Ditto potatoes, because of the starch. *Very unhelpful.* Essentially, sugar was to be avoided although some fruits with a low glycogen index could be taken in *absolutely minimal amounts.* Say half an apple every few days, but certainly no bananas or citrus fruits, which were *known to be damaging. Did that mean that wine* – I began… Alcohol was absolutely forbidden. *Could red wine… reservatrols…?* I mentioned vaguely. She shook her head, and I saw a look of disbelief that I would suggest such a dangerous and harmful thing as a drink if I wanted to save my husband's life. Did she not realise I hadn't bought any wine for at least a month at this point, so we weren't tempted? I was desperate for a drink myself and had thought I was doing my bit. After an hour and a half she left, and that night sent through a list of 22 supplements, pills and tinctures which Andrew was to begin taking immediately. She advised me precisely on a centrifugal juicer, its make and series number, and why nothing else would be as effective. We could lose a further 20–30 per cent of the essential vitamins and minerals were we to buy another make. She seemed a kind, good woman and I knew she was the least likely person to be trying to sell me anything or make money out of our misfortune, yet I also felt mystified by much of what she had said, and disbelieving.

The next morning I went online to buy the tinctures, pills and powders she had prescribed, and then, finding myself baffled by whether or not I had the right compound of magnesium and selenium, began walking around our kitchen, where nothing felt safe any more. I began to throw away the tins and packets I had always thought I might use one day. I threw the ingredients my sons and I used to bake cakes with – they were always badly iced, often a little burnt, but Andrew loved being presented with them. Out went the white flour and the caster sugar (*both cancer stimulating*). I flung the non-organic eggs and bags of salad (*very bad*), the dried fruit (*sugar*), the coffee (*toxic*), the tea (*caffeine*), a pineapple (*acidic*) into the bin, without even bothering to recycle any of it. I was furious and it was bullshit, but *it was all poisonous and would do him further harm, studies showed.*

Yet I also felt seized by panic that I would be at fault and have only myself to blame if I could not get this right for him. His diet. The least I could do. An enlarged sense of responsibility that turned to guilt quickly. The sense of getting something wrong, doing something badly and causing harm. My own internal saboteur was out and about again but I felt desperate to help Andrew however I could.

This included arranging to meet our widowed neighbour for coffee on Marylebone High Street. In that strange first week back at work in January, I bumped into as were letting ourselves through our front doors one day. We didn't know her well, but she had been friendly, and I respected how she had dealt with her husband's death.

I disclosed the news over the slim railings almost by accident. Perhaps she could discern, in that way that I now can, that something was wrong. We had been meant to be at the same place one day and Andrew and I had not turned up.

Everything OK? Her key was poised at her door.

For some reason I told her that Andrew had had to have a small procedure.

Nothing worrying? She tilted her head and looked at me very directly.

Well, actually, no. It's just last week, he... er... yes. He's got cancer.

Let's meet and chat, she offered, in a straightforward way. I did not tell him of the meeting I'd arranged by text with her later.

Look, I am sure he will be absolutely fine, the neighbour said, two days later, smiling, a cup of mint tea poised in her hands. The airy space of the café we were sat in muted the sound of her voice so that I, on the other side of the small table had to lean forward and turn my head to hear. I did not want to miss a word.

I could not afford to miss a word.

It was one of those very dry January mornings. The roads branching off left to right were slightly frosted, breath visible everywhere as shoppers converged on the Conran Shop, Waitrose and Daunt Books on their way down to Oxford Street. The sales. We sat in the window of the café at the top of the street, four lanes of traffic humming past on the Marylebone Road. Her own husband had died eighteen months before, of a vicious, symptom-heavy cancer. This had transformed her, helpfully for me, into an expert on the subject. In the first twenty minutes, she named the masseuses, physiotherapists, acupuncturists and reflexologists available to assist in the new world we would be living in. She spoke assuredly of the vibrant soft market that surrounds cancer. That it was really essential to tap into. *These things really make a difference. There is a lot of evidence that it really does work you know. Things are changing and reversing the disease for lots of people. Really, they are. Incredible results.* I felt stunned by her generosity and optimism actually. Her husband was dead; how did any of this work or make any difference? Why was she asserting the benefits so enthusiastically to me? And as she spoke, I felt my mood picking up, my hope returning that maybe this was all sort-able, with the right people, the right *support.* This woman knew exactly what she was talking about and I was lucky that I had let her in on the secret. We had money to throw at the problem and yes, I could make the difference. She continued, an endless list of thoughtful suggestions. *Organisation and the right people.* She smiled again kindly and we both looked at our watches.

What she described is, in reality, a market for desperate people of means that her listener would soon think is unregulated, total nonsense and an utter waste of time. I still do. To clarify – for people with fatal cancers like Andrew, although not for others, who will benefit greatly, in many ways.

And in the months to come, he half-heartedly submitted to some of these 'complementary' treatments because I think he thought it made me feel better. She waited patiently as I checked through my carefully jotted notes and looked up at her, one last question about accupunture in my mind. Then I heard her say, *a second opinion.*

I felt my temperature rise sharply.

What do you mean?

Well, you know, B would be alive today if he hadn't got so in thrall to the surgeon here. If he had gone to Sloan, the best cancer hospital in New York, he would still be alive. Had he found the right guy here – who was there all along, still is, Sloan Kettering, doing the op, he would still be alive. So what harm can it do? I would certainly make sure that I had one. Get a second opinion. The States lead in so much of this. Add that to the list.

The neighbour put her head to one side. *You'll get the*

best possible care here, but it can't do any harm to have another option – should... everything go pear shaped. Which it won't. She smiled again, looked at me, then turned away and sipped at her tea.

Another fastidious smile and brisk shoulder shrug. I felt agonised for her. She was sad-eyed, mid-career, a mother of three young sons. Yet there was no anger or resentment in her generous donation of the best names for cranial people and back guys, vitamin C IV drips and a wonderful Polish homeopath. Lastly, several tubes of unused aloe vera gel were produced from her handbag.

Essential for post-radiotherapy skin. It should be fine to use still – yes, in fact... another thirteen months to go. She put her glasses on the end of her nose to read the label. *So... let's see. Right. Yes. Perfect. B found it very good. Very soothing.* Another smile as she laid them on the table.

The meeting was over.

Thank you for all your help. I can't tell you how helpful you've been, I said, my hand on her arm. I didn't feel this at all, though. I felt strange. Even more unarmed and vulnerable. A second opinion. The US. America? Really? The neighbour proffered her cheek and we set off in different directions, until I heard her voice again. I turned around, hopefully, wondering if from now we would be friends and she wanted to meet again. I wanted to hold onto her.

Just remember, if you have any doubts, a second opinion. Make sure you get it. She waved and turned away.

I took her late husband's gel home and put it into my side of the bathroom cabinet, behind a box of paracetamol. I always noticed the tubes, though, every so often pushed behind shampoo and conditioner miniatures picked up on hotel trips. And that the expiry date on them was February 2015.

Andrew was, I saw, giving me control of his diet, and the very few complementary appointments he acquiesced to – but everything else was taken back. I saw him as I had never seen him in the first few months, felt how it might have been to be opposite him in a business deal. I had never expected to be on this other side.

Life went on as normal, however, and he told me often that this was his illness and he would make his own choices. I would not have dared disobey.

Before he was ill, I frequently heard him say to people, *We decide everything together, we love to. We don't do anything without agreeing it.* And for me too, this was true. I loved the shared home of our mind as well as our actual home. We loved deciding together and then presenting our decision to others. We loved the fact we needed no one but each other. We were quite omnipotent, I see that now, as good couples often are; it is one of the perks. You take each other into account before other people. We practiced a shutting out of outside views, when necessary, a looking after our relationship and the responsibilities that we had to each other. Yet the balance had started to shift.

No, no one is to know. Do you understand? When one night at the very end of January I gingerly asked if I could tell another person for very good reasons, he was unhappy, disconsolate, disappointed with me. *Why do you need to? I just want to get back to normal. Really, no one needs to know. Please, it is going to be over and what will have been the point of telling everyone?*

How could I not comply?

9

Best Men

Wasi had returned from his Christmas break in Mumbai by the time Andrew was due to begin treatment. I knew Andrew was relieved Wasi was back and we met him to discuss the fact that Andrew would get the best possible people to care for him. After the appointment in Wasi's room at the London Clinic, I commented to Andrew that there couldn't be just one best man, surely, where were the best women and also, surely *everyone* would want the best man? Andrew didn't smile, didn't like my sense of humour. The 'best man' was another part of the way in which cancer had to be spoken of, and part of the delusion. I quickly learnt that when discussing his treatment with both our families I too would frequently use the same term. Mr Altman was definitely *the best man for the job*, I heard myself saying after we were introduced to this smiling man, about my age.

Mr Altman was a radiotherapist (a strangely old-fashioned-sounding term) and told Andrew at our first meeting he believed he could eradicate the tumour.

Boasted, at times I have unkindly thought, that he could take it away. Andrew, sitting upright with his hands clasped tightly in front of him, asked him to repeat the word.

So you're saying eradicate?

Yes, I am saying that is what I hope to do.

OK, good. He slowly nodded his head. *Good. Honestly?*

Now I believe that every doctor we met in the first six months was so intimidated by my husband that they could barely face telling him the facts. Mr Altman was Andrew's key consultant in the first six months of his fourteen-month illness. The person who would tell him the treatment had not been successful, six months later. I have reflected a great deal about how Andrew ran the appointments with this pale young oncologist like board meetings. I noticed how often he bowed his head to him, so we were left looking at Mr Altman's incongruous black kippah in his high-tech office as we peered over the digital scans of Andrew's left lung.

From the first time we met him, for the initial diagnosis of the first scan, to the series of planning meetings, as they are called, that followed, I always felt he could not wait to get us out of the room. Mr Altman was pleasant and warm to us both, but while I simply wanted to hear what he had to say, take his instructions, make the next appointment and leave, Andrew had other ideas. At each appointment, once Mr Altman had described the situation concerning the tumour, Andrew wanted to have a discussion. But it wasn't clarification or another explanation, but an agreement, that he seemed to be seeking. As if Mr Altman needed to be negotiated with, for a deal to be done. I sat there feeling uncomfortable and embarrassed, wondering why Andrew could not see what I could. There was no joint venture here, no successful negotiation to be done, nothing to be brokered and managed. Andrew could not win here. There was simply a fact, and a need for submission to the treatment, as prescribed.

Who was the bloody doctor in there? I asked one day when we left after another 'planning' meeting. *What do you mean?* Andrew said, hurt, looking at me as we went down in the tiny lift.

Despite Andrew's substantial commitment and insurance payments to private healthcare policies over the years, we were worried and frustrated at the time the treatment took to get started. Throughout January, he seemed to be sent for endless tests, while each visit to Mr Altman involved looking at different images, such as the radar screen outlining where the radiotherapy lasers would presumably blast through the tumour. All our plans had been changed and the 40 or so days and nights seemed to drag endlessly, weekends feeling like wasted time, when nothing happened, but the cancer was still growing. Six weeks after the initial diagnosis, so by now mid-February, just as the radiotherapy was about to start, Andrew was recalled. It seemed an MRI scan had detected some new and strange lesions on his spine.

Our first consultant, the young lung physician, had insisted on more information, so someone even better, another best person in London, had been asked to analyse the latest scan. Wasi called us in and together we sat listening to him. He seemed edgy and a little anxious. The results had strangely come back as non-diagnosable. They were on balance, fairly sure, he said, that this was just related to Andrew's long history of sport- and golf-ragged spine. Wasi reassured us and said he was pretty sure too, and then Andrew reminded us both that 40 years of swings fucked everyone's spines and the three of us laughed, briefly. Wasi quickly added, however, that as a precaution, and at the request of the lung physician, they thought a visit to the Royal Marsden would be sensible.

Andrew shook his head incredulously.

What? I watched Wasi look down as Andrew frowned, looking critically at the doctor's tilted head. *Really, Wasi, is that really necessary? I mean, we have a plan, we know what we're doing, we've got Altman who's the best there is. Do we seriously need to see someone else for another opinion?*

Wasi's phone rang and he looked embarrassed. Andrew motioned for him to pick it up. *OK, thank you, yes, I am just finishing. Please tell him I'll see him shortly.* Andrew sighed, shook his head and stood up, holding his hand out to him.

Fine, whatever you say, Wasi, you know I trust you completely. As you suggest, it's sensible, belt and braces, but I don't think they are going to find anything else. I know my body. It's 40 years of thousands of golf swings, of course it's going to be fucked. He smiled warmly at the doctor. *Onwards, Wasi, just get them to get me in there today, will you?* Wasi smiled.

I'll do my best, Andrew, of course.

Wasi made the right calls, and the next day we found ourselves waiting in another doctor's consulting room, this time on the lower-ground floor of the Royal Marsden, a large brick hospital on the Fulham Road. Unlike the terraces of Harley Street, the Marsden is a forbidding building, claggy with pollution and somehow oddly positioned amid the expensive wallpaper and interiors shops of SW7.

The professor we had come to meet was the world lead on lung-cancer-related spinal matters, Andrew told me as we sat waiting. I understood this to mean he was an expert on lung tumours that metastasise, that spread, but nodded. *That's great. Good for Wasi. Well done, sweetheart.* Andrew was straight-backed, alert and handsome in a dark-navy cord jacket and jeans, a white shirt open at the neck and his hands clasped between his open legs, as if ready to spring.

The professor was shown into the room by a nurse a few minutes after us. He was a small, rotund and brisk man. We stood up to shake his hand and while Andrew was not discourteous, it was soon evident to me that he did not want to be there. We sat in silence as the professor matter-of-factly told us that he thought the marking on the lower part of Andrew's back and pelvis were indications of metastatic spread. Andrew immediately began to argue with him, to explain that his golf swing was to blame, his spine had been excessively used, he had already in his thirties and forties had issues with two of the discs, and this was nothing new. But the professor was having none of his explan-ations. After a few minutes, Andrew gave up and sat back in the chair while the doctor weighed up his thoughts in front of us, his head bowed over a sheaf of blood results and photographs of Andrew's lower vertebrae, tapping his nails either side of his blotting pad.

Look, I'm sorry. I was given these this morning and I had them fit you in, but I haven't had as much time as I would like. He did not look up, but continued moving the scans around on the illuminated screen built into the desk, occasionally looking left to the typed paperwork. Andrew rolled his eyes and looked at me. The room was completely quiet, the double glazing insulating against the busy traffic. Three double-deckers filed past. Eventually, the doctor looked up, his dark-brown eyes narrow, frowning at us. He shrugged his shoulders and hesitated, then began to speak.

On balance, normally this would be a sign the cancer has got into the bone, but I'm not entirely sure. It is unusual. My view is... I think it has spread. It's not possible to be conclusive, but all my experience – well...

He looked at his watch, and then up again at us. He was sorry, but perfunctory. For the first time I felt we were not being soft-soaped with tactful ambiguity. He smiled, his lips together, and looked at me, then at Andrew again, almost quizzically, and stood up. He said he had ordered another radiotherapist to take a look and the results would be back within 48 hours, and we should ask our GP to chase them if they weren't. Andrew was polite, curt and contained during the last two minutes of the consultation as I thanked the doctor and we shook hands. As we left the building, Andrew began to storm up the Fulham Road. I let him go ahead of me, and he walked for 50 metres before turning around and looking at me, his hands outstretched in front of him and his dark coat flapping out in the chilly February sun. *I'm sorry. But what a cunt. There should be a law against people saying things like that. Fucking hell.* He took his glasses off and rubbed the bridge of his nose, his way of telling me when he felt overwhelmed. However, he insisted we go for lunch. At the restaurant, I stared at the table, unable to look at him as I felt I would start crying uncontrollably. But half an hour later, he was coming up again, almost buoyant, shaking his head as he deftly ate a huge bowl of minestrone in front of me, sipping fast at a large glass of red wine, tearing pieces of bread and eating them hungrily, ignoring my wheat and alcohol ban. Not that I cared that day.

He doesn't know what he's talking about, not a clue. It has not one hundred per cent spread, sweetheart, I know it.

I sat meekly in silence, awed by his confidence but horrified again by what was going on, by what we had just been told. I had disappointed my younger son again, leaving him in tears that morning by missing his class concert to be with Andrew. I felt guiltily about how much I wished I was in the bright overheated junior school listening to him scratching away at his viola.

The next morning, we returned to the young consultant we had run to on the night of the diagnosis, to be told that the scan was inconclusive.

We would therefore be pressing on with the original plan of 40 daily sessions of radiotherapy to his chest, followed by eight sessions of chemotherapy to his body, 'the belt and braces approach', to get rid of this cancer. Andrew banged the table and covered his face with his palms for a second. This was the only time I saw him cry, briefly and with his hand over his forehead, the other gripping the arm of the chair in the doctor's large bland consulting room. He searched for my hand and I got up and hugged him. The doctor looked on, and then away. His iPhone lay on the table between us, its cover a photograph of the two little kids I had seen that first night back in December. He got up. Andrew breathed deeply and stood up.

The doctor took his hand and shook it. *I just want to wish you the best of luck. We'll stay in touch, of course. You've got the best people. Promise.*

We left and Andrew seemed ecstatic, vindicated. *You see, I knew, I knew it was nothing to do with the disease. I knew it.* We walked home, the now familiar route, the morning dry and freezing, both this time with coats, gloves, scarves. We were prepared.

In the next few days, I would hear him say to those few friends who knew, to our families, *I was so, so lucky to have this one* – a kiss on my head – *and second-to-none medical care – plus acupuncture and kale, for fuck's sake. That's all she's let me eat over the last month.* His hand clutching mine, toasting his lucky escape. I winced as I heard him say this and I wince now. *I was so lucky, I can't imagine what it would be like to hear the news we were fortunate enough not to be given. When the doctor said – it looks as if it hasn't spread anywhere, we can't see it anywhere else – God. The feeling, amazing. I wept, the only time.* He looked at me and smiled, I smiled back. *I prayed, for Christ's sake.*

He had indeed started to pray. I often think now about his quiet return to prayer during those months. He would hang back before appointments; did I mind, he asked, but he wanted to say the *Shema*, the most important Jewish prayer, *shema* meaning hear or listen. The prayer, recited twice or more a day by very religious Jews, affirms the covenant with God, that they will follow His rules and that in return God will take care of them. No wonder he started to say it again; it is a beautiful-sounding recitation, soothing in its rhythm and familiarity. Andrew was both rejecting and embracing of his Judaism, and I could never predict when some element of his Orthodox childhood would reappear, some moment when he would say a word to me in Yiddish, smirking with laughter at what a great word it was, or call me *bubbelah* instead of sweetheart. Nor could I predict when he would order a plate of Parma ham, patting his stomach, or grimace if we went somewhere and were offered roast pork. Once, early on, he told me he was intellectually comfortable with his Judaism, but not spiritually, but I felt it was much more complicated than that. However, now, during these days, he often spoke in his elegant and fluent Hebrew, and asked for healing of his soul, and body.

Of course I don't mind, whatever you want to say or do is what I want, I said, when he asked me what I thought of his prayers.

In those spring months, I would wait for him on the twisting staircase leading up to Mr Altman's office, moved and wanting to hear him, or when we went for his doses of chemotherapy, stopping by the lift while he prayed. I would hear him on the stairs in our tall thin house, whispering in Hebrew, a mother tongue of sorts, a language learnt as a small boy. Yet his tallit (or prayer shawl) lived in a plastic crate above his wardrobe, along with other remnants from his bar mitzvah. He was asking for help in a way I had never known him to in our time together. Who knows. (He would not be buried in his tallit as it was in the wrong country when he died.) I was relieved and pleased by his prayers. I hoped it would help. Freud, the Godless Jew as he called himself, saw religion as a reversion to childish patterns of thought in response to feelings of helplessness and guilt. Humans frequently experience insecurity and crave absolution and so they create God. He regarded belief as a childish delusion and atheism as an adult reality. Religion, for Andrew, was complex and yet urgent now. He had rejected it after a childhood of enforcement, but now, in an overwhelming need for reassurance, he took it up again. He felt listened to in his prayers and not doubted. At some level I think he felt I didn't believe him. And he was, in part, right.

Yet, that crisp February morning Andrew accepted this final opinion – inconclusive – because he had a version of this illness and it suited him. He could not countenance a change to the plan, to the lie, really, because it might have prevented us from carrying on. Someone else might have said inconclusive wasn't good enough. But not him.

However, my doubts began again to multiply. It wasn't that it wasn't there; it was that the scans were 'inconclusive'. There was something there, some change in the bones in his spine but just not the kind of change that could be labelled as cancer related to the type in his lung or his neck. But that morning, as we walked home again from the consultant and his good news, Portland Place sunlit, red buses, black cabs, the usual fleet of unusually smart cars that cruise W1, and a cloudless sky hanging over Regent's Park, Andrew was swinging my hand in the air. The lump in his neck was about to be nuked, so that would mean it was gone and then there was just the lung bit to deal with. Rudimentary, binary. Nietzsche, not a psychoanalyst but sounding like one in *Beyond Good and Evil* (1886), asks, *Suppose we want truth: why not rather untruth? And uncertainty? Even ignorance?* Nietzsche asks what is the point of having to live, if we cannot live with illusions? This must include the illusion that we and those we love won't die. Was this lying, or hope?

I never did disclose to Andrew that I had developed a habit of googling stories of people with lung cancer and discovered that it was not *ever* curable. The illusions,

though – the best man in London, the fact that inconclusive meant nothing, the prayers – all these were ways
in which I think he wanted me to help him hold the
tremendous and unavoidable anxiety away from him.
He wanted to manipulate me to think the way he insisted
on thinking, and I fell in with this wish. We both knew it
was a terrible, appalling disease that he had contracted,
but this could not be said. It was critical that it was not
said. It had to be minimised, spoken of only in terms of
the treatment, not the horror of its inevitable outcome.

So, he didn't ignore his cancer. The opposite. He
diligently committed to and got on with the treatment.
He followed the strict diet I imposed, he submitted
to acupuncture, once tried yoga, and renounced anti-
perspirant sprays completely, as well as his favourite
toothpaste, soap and dry skin cream, because none of
them were organic and *might kill him*. All of this he
gave up, as he also split off the idea that the cancer might
not go away, might be untreatable. Terminal. He denied
the thought. And so death... death. This remained an
unthinkable and obscene concept for us both during the
fourteen months. It became as unthinkable a thought
as your parents having sex to make you, or as a parent
yourself, wanting to actually murder your own child.

'Splitting' is a term used in psychoanalysis to describe
a defence mechanism, when someone has to literally 'get
rid' of a thought which cannot be tolerated, to substitute
it with another, often in opposition. It is characteristic
of those who can't live with greyness and uncertainty.
With us, it meant we could not simultaneously maintain

the possibility of both surviving and not surviving the disease. The only way we could cope was to deny the reality of the cancer and keep it as far away from our conscious minds as it could be. We both did, the exception for me being during my analysis sessions when I would raise the possibility of Andrew's death and listen to the analyst's silence, his lack of response to my need for him to tell me it would be all right. And it was no comfort to me at all. It was, however, the truth.

Yet at the same time, Andrew and I were closer than ever, more solicitous than ever of each other. The separations were hard, sometimes an hour felt painful, and I admired him for his ability to both carry on as normal and be able to tell me he needed me. We went to work as usual. We met for lunch as often as my patients allowed and he would leave his office early to be with me as soon as I had breaks between patients. *I need to see you if it is only for ten minutes* (the time I allowed between sessions). We had always tolerated separation badly, but one night in early March I felt I had to go to a close friend's 40th birthday dinner, even though it meant leaving him alone, as he had had chemotherapy the day before and had gone to bed as soon as he got home from work. Chemotherapy progressively gets worse and he had succumbed to how wretched he felt this time. The guilt and misery overwhelmed me and I returned early. He was awake and almost tearful in bed. *How could you leave me for two hours? How could you do that? How, how, how?*

I told him honestly that not only had I felt I should

go, but I wanted to. That I needed some oxygen, that no one knew that he was ill, that it was Kate's birthday, and that I needed to be among my friends even if I could not tell them what was happening. Even if I could not tell them Andrew had been diagnosed with lung cancer and was lying at home in bed, on day three of his second chemotherapy cycle, day nineteen of radiotherapy. When Kate asked, I said he was at a business dinner and had sent his apologies. He was inconsolable and angry for longer than felt bearable.

All of this sounds bizarre and naive to me years later, now he is dead, but at the time, it was, simply, our life. You live believing you will continue to live. I agreed to his rules because he was sick; he was the one suffering, not me. Of course, those who love an ill person suffer too, just differently, but my life was not threatened with oblivion.

And it kept us psychically contained.

I won't write about the side effects of the treatments, and in any case he wanted to ignore them. He was very brave indeed. He was also fit, and this probably helped, but it is all relative. Chemotherapy is a brutal, primitive act of violence against the body, a Cif-like scouring of the system. He somehow got through it, quietly, invisibly, but so did the tumours, now beginning to rapidly procreate, dodging the flow of the chemicals through his veins, sucking themselves into corners, rendering themselves tiny, imperceptible. How clever they were. And how utterly uncomplaining he was.

10

Unconscious Residues

And life continued.

It could be reduced to something like this: two toothbrushes, one leaning to the left, and one to the right, in a tumbler, by a sink. Or the way he folds and places his clothes nightly, meekly even, over the armchair in our bedroom, while I leave mine between our bathroom and the wardrobe, over the bath, sometimes hanging on a hook, generally not. Jeans, socks, whatever I take off. A shoe here. A shoe there. Inside-out jersey on the floor. He shakes his head and smiles when he gets into bed. He never tires of it. *I love your messiness. I love it. You do make me laugh.* He works to pass an arm underneath my side in our bed and holds me. *You feel so lovely.* As tiny and pathetic as that.

Your life lived as a couple, as two people who fill a space together, who rely on each other, who love each other.

Who, every night, alone in the dark in their bed, were back together again. *What a joy,* we would say to each other. *What an absolute bloody joy. You're here.*

Four long months of treatment were followed by a

final procedure and in the summer, finally, an apparent all-clear. Were we happy, relieved? I can't remember; yes, I think we felt something was better and yet the fact that it is so foggy suggests to me that I didn't perhaps believe we were out of the woods. We had a lot to do, a lot to distract us, work, our new house, the summer break looming. We got back to getting on. We had planned from the beginning of our relationship that we would get married and so we chose a day, coinciding with the end of the treatment. It was a lovely afternoon. The sun burnt through the glass roof of the room we were married in, on a Friday, in the countryside. My aunt, a theologian, came and talked to us the week before and unwove and explained the Song of Songs for me, helped by Andrew. Then, on the day, my two cousins took turns to read it. Jewish and Christian commentators have interpreted it as being about God's relationship with his people, but as for thousands of other couples on their wedding day, it spoke to us of what we felt. *Let him kiss me with the kisses of his mouth; for your love is better than wine.* Andrew smiled at me, then looked down, his eyes rimmed with tears. I felt immensely excited, as if life were full of promise. I remember wondering why he could be crying. When, in his open, poignant speech at the wedding supper, he conveyed his gratitude that I had stood by his side through this nightmare, I couldn't understand why he spent so much time talking about his illness. I looked around the room, at our family and closest friends gathered there, and felt – joy. The rest of his speech was also funny, direct and clever. I was so proud and impressed by him. I also think now that I managed to deny the reality for the entire weekend. My capacity to 'split' was growing.

And Andrew's cancer continued to be almost *completely* symptom-free from diagnosis until the end of summer, a full eight months. Astonishing, perhaps, but true. No cough, no breathlessness, absolutely nothing. But a nagging back pain had begun in late August while we were on holiday in Italy. We were staying with Italian friends on the coast near Livorno when the pain became really terrible. They suggested he visit an osteopath who had helped my friend with a bad back injury. We ventured into the hot city centre one afternoon to meet the quiet tanned man in a short-sleeved white medic's coat. Andrew asked me to sit in on the consultation to explain in Italian what was wrong. He also told me not to tell the osteopath he had had cancer, and I remember rolling my eyes and scowling at him. Of course I was going to tell him he had had cancer. *No, no,* he insisted, holding my wrist as we climbed up the cool marble staircase, past the offices of a cardiac surgeon and a psychiatrist. *Because it isn't relevant. I've just got back pain, and that, nothing else, is what I want him to sort out.* I complied as the osteopath peered at Andrew's shoulders. Gently, he asked Andrew to lie down and watched as he winced in pain. After five minutes, he advised me that something was *'molto inflammato'*, which he couldn't get to in only one session, and suggested we buy some ibuprofen gel en route back to our villa. Andrew spent the rest of the week heavily dosed on painkillers.

Stewart and Camilla had come to stay with us with their sons in the place we had rented the next week in the countryside, and while we attempted to enjoy the Tuscan heat, something felt amiss. I recently found footage on my phone of an evening in a pizzeria, where my older son filmed Andrew being interviewed on what pizza was best, but his face is not as I remember him with us, open and amused by childish humour, but rather, drawn and tired, wanting them to stop, wanting to go home. Wanting pain relief. The week ended at the airport with him shouting at a check-in assistant and agreeing with me that even if he was convinced the pain was related to his golf swing, we should go and see Wasi on our return. He made an appointment for first thing the next day, at which Wasi recommended a spinal steroid injection.

We had (of course) been referred to another *best* person. This time it was a frosty Australian who called himself a pain relief consultant. Wasi claimed the Australian's skill with backs brought quivering wrecks of *strong guys like you* back to normal life with a long injection into their withered bulging vertebrae.

I saw how the consultant nodded as he ran through a few questions about his golf playing. Andrew sat back, legs apart, and began to gesture and talk about his game as the consultant studied the murky scan shots, clicking them around the screen.

I did not warm to him and watched as he listened, bored, tapping his fingers as Andrew, practised by now, gave him his lengthy explanation.

Too much golf, the pain was very familiar, suffered it for years, this was nothing new. If only he could get rid of this bloody back pain, life would be good. No other symptoms. He'd coasted through radio- and chemotherapy and this was just boring. We had another scan coming up mid-September but it seemed that the thing was gone, blasted away. Just this pain. It's golf. Everyone messes their spine up if they play it enough.

A cold smile across the desk. I could see Andrew didn't think that the Australian believed his story. He wasn't interested in him, and said little, but agreed to inject him the next week.

Great, fantastic. I'm really so grateful. Andrew took his hand with both of his and shook hard. *I know I can take it, I've had this pain for years.*

Even though I said nothing, I felt that there was something else wrong with his back, and that the Australian knew this too. I felt I knew that the back pain was connected with the unspeakable thing inside him, that despite the months of radiotherapy, the chemotherapy, the scans showing some apparent progress, some stabilisation, some reduction, some retraction, there was nothing to say it had gone away. Andrew had what in the consulting room I would think of as a 'negative transference' to the consultant. He felt dismissed by him, disbelieved, which reminded him of every other person who had made him feel that way. I don't think Andrew was used to feeling like this, mainly because since early adolescence he had made every effort to overcome anyone who attempted to put him down, or didn't respect his views. But a primitive super-ego was in the room with us that day, telling him he wasn't good enough, that he could be outsmarted. That he was desperate and that he had to beg people to cure him. That is what cancer does, makes you feel pathetic, urgent, grateful. That evening we would have supper together, once the boys were in bed, and now, with the autumn coming, and somehow the prospect of the anniversary of his diagnosis reappearing, our conversations could be different. Would I bring up his illness, or wait for him to not mention it? I avoided it.

But to my unconscious, so much part of my professional and most private life, the thought of something else, death, did come, had come, often, since that afternoon of the diagnosis. The thought was a fragile, hesitant thing. The thought often returned at night, hugging the waist of my unconscious, like a monkey refusing to let go of its mother, in my dreams.

It is not possible he will die until we know that he will die. We are nowhere near that, I would say to myself over and over and over again that year, through the day, when it sneaked back as I hunted for a pack of 6–8-year-old pants for my son in John Lewis, or sat ankles crossed in my consulting room waiting for my 1pm patient, or washed shampoo out of my hair.

The active thought never came when I was with Andrew. His realness confounded the fear. There was all that life in his body. His legs on the car seat next to me, my hand on his thigh as he drove. My eyes on his as he kissed me. His dark skull hovering over me late at night. His even breathing, matching his easy descent into sleep. The feeling of safety I had in a room with him.

This is the strange thing. The normality. The utter, unchanging normality. The sound of him showering, sipping his tea, on the phone to his business partner, his sneeze, his Jackie Mason jokes about how little was in the fridge, his laughter watching something sent to him on his iPad, his pinching my bottom as I went up the stairs. His careful and forensic reading of the *Financial Times* every day, by 7.15am. His interest in everything, towns and cities and buildings in particular (his work was in this field), but also in ideas, economics, theatre, stories, politics, how you could do things differently. He listened carefully to people – I saw that early on; he never pronounced. His thorough enjoyment of being alive.

There were too all the huge and small ways he made me love him, which constantly added to his aliveness. How could someone who provoked so much in me not live? Andrew had run a company with thousands of employees for many years before I met him. He was completely self-made, extremely hard-working and had worked his way up alone. I was impressed by him; I wanted to be like him. Early on in our friendship, I saw him give a speech that was fluent and poised, and having greeted me, he took off to work a room of several hundred people. I watched him going round, neatly beginning and leaving conversations, charming, establishing eye contact, with firm handshakes and pats on the back. But once (two years or so later) we were together, I found many contradictions. He told me (and I saw) how shy he was. He liked to follow me into a party or supper where we might meet new people, for example, telling me I was much better at that sort of thing. He was, like most people, subject to conflicts. Calling himself Jewish and a businessman, but hating the term a Jewish businessman. He had unresolved and dismissive feelings about the faith of his childhood and yet felt and was unmistakeably Jewish. He loathed certain terms, and was horrified when a non-Jewish friend of mine jokingly used the word '*shiksah*', as he knew it to be a deeply insulting term to use for a woman. He rolled his eyes at the idea of being a member of a chosen people, but his face was chastened and sad on the night of Kol Nidre – although he refused to go to synagogue on Yom Kippur. He was fiercely protective of Israel but thought its politics nationalistic, militaristic and aggressive. He was furious with his old synagogue for many reasons, and in particular with someone there he had lent money who had never repaid him. He harboured grudges and could not move forward from arguments. He had very few close friends when I met him but didn't want to make many more. While business and deals came naturally to him, friendship did not. He had been hurt and let down by people, he said. I saw how he provoked envy in people but didn't understand it. He was vulnerable and thin-skinned despite his audacious career. But he had me.

And I was completely fascinated by him. By his boyish contradictions; faced with a menu, wanting things that he described as *'bad for me'* – but then asking me to decide for him: *Love – would this be better or that be better for me?* By his ease in the chaos of an airport, his careful, rather slow driving, but refusal to wear a seat belt, his excitement in a vexing business problem, but similarly frustration that made him throw phones at the wall. By the patterns of numbers he jotted down on endless pieces of paper, sitting down suddenly to write them as if an equation had come into his head. I was transfixed by the self-belief he had when something *I knew* was not going to happen, and yet actually did happen due to his dogged persistence that enabled him to turn around a situation. The pleasure I saw in his eyes when I put a new pair of jeans on and he asked me to turn slowly around in them, *twice please*. His patient listening to his sons' long phone calls about their work and his careful advice. His decisiveness. His deep pride in all his children's achievements. His delight when he spoke to certain people on the phone, the funny voice, the accents, loud gunfire laughter. His rapid kick of a ball with my boys in the garden. His inability to make anything other than a cup of tea or toast. His singing along loudly to his music. His lack of fear of anyone. His care for me, his worry about me, his intense wish for me to be happy. His biting his lower lip if he felt I was angry with him. *Oh God – what is it? Have I upset you?* His urgent, vulnerable self. How he told me he needed me to love him. Him telling me he would actually kill anyone who tried to harm me or the children. All this smacked of life. Of a long and enduring life.

Yet alongside all this life, I recognised there was much more going on in the dark depths of my mind. I could only confess to it in my analysis. My nocturnal unconscious landscape was full of it, full of being alone and deeply worried. A recurrent nightmare began of a former boyfriend lurking around some cavernous institution which I found myself in, forcing me to hide. A prison, a borstal-like place of my imagination. Once I slid gasping down the inside of a door while he looked for me through the wired glass square above me. His familiar sing-song mocking voice: *Where are you? I am here, I know where you are. Don't think you can hide. I can see you.* Something was happening, I was beginning to feel threatened and scared. A search for someone, Andrew, to protect me, who could not be found in this strange, medicalised, inhospitable place of my internal world. He was still alive, though; he wasn't going anywhere. No one had told us otherwise.

11

Repression

I woke up terrified one night.

By this point, the treatment had long ended. It was October and a storm was threatening somewhere to the west of the city, marking the change in temperature after that indecently hot September. We were in bed early, both of us tired and falling quickly into silence, holding hands and me listening for his steady exhalation before losing consciousness myself, a habit that had become essential to my own sleep. That night, though, I woke with a falling feeling and a cry, beating the wide mattress with my palm trying to find him. In the blackness Andrew asked me what was wrong and hugged me, but I could not say. *Just a horrid bad dream.* I cowered in his arms, still damp with shock. I had woken him up with two very shrill shrieks, he said, and pulled me to him.

Our old windows were by now shaking in the strong winds blowing across the park from the west, and a gale broke against the tall stucco house. It was raining, but it did not feel reassuring or comforting any more in our bed. The traffic still ground past on the Euston Road and the noise of the trees in the park brought the outside in. Alongside us now, as well as the cancer separating us, were a series of silent, invisible impositions that only we could see. Something deeply buried and repressed had woken me up to reality from the depths of sleep. He hugged me tightly.

It will be all right, nothing bad is going to happen. I am the exception to the rule. You know. We know that. I love you. I will never ever leave you. I have found you, and you have found me. This is it. No one is taking us away from each other.

I felt his kiss on my nose, and nodded, by then lying with my back to him, his arms solid around me.

He sounded like someone lying to his mistress.

The fear was beginning to penetrate me, to become internalised. 'Internalisation' is a term used in psychoanalysis to describe the mechanism by which a feeling becomes part of someone's personality. It can have both a positive and a negative connotation. I might think of a strong super-ego, in a patient who easily hears a harsh, critical (possibly parental) voice that tells them that they are worthless or doing something badly or wrong.

So what I mean is that I began to know from this point more and more consciously that the illness was much more powerful than he, or I, or the treatment, and therefore that we were no longer in control. The dream woke me up, and I screamed, conscious finally, that I had something to be utterly terrified of.

I waited until I heard his even, light breathing. This man who could sleep with an incubus inside him.

How did he manage it?

On walks that autumn, around the park, I would conjure sadistic fantasies for myself, imagine getting back home and him not being there. The sitting room without him, the kitchen where he would never go again. I would only stay for a few minutes in this dark new place, as someone in the world without him. Were these my adult games of Fort Da? Freud's famous story illustrated his theory of the Pleasure Principle. In 1919, he began to observe his eighteen-month-old grandson, Little Ernst, the son of Sophie, his favourite daughter. Ernst was a baby deeply attached to his mother. Unusually for the times, Sophie had fed and cared for him with the help of only one maid. Freud described his observation of Sophie leaving Ernst. After a moment's distress, Ernst began a strange little game. He would take great pleasure in throwing his toys as far as he could from himself, in effect, hiding them from himself, and then diligently refinding them again. As he threw he would shout *Fort!*, sounding like *Gone!* in German, and *Da!* (*There!*) A mother's absences are never pleasurable for a young child, although often necessary. Recovering the lost bobbin Ernst liked to play with anticipated the pleasure he would experience when she returned to him. I had developed my own repetition compulsion for the person I needed the most. I would practise throwing Andrew away, knowing I would return to find him. I must have known his absence was drawing nearer.

In those months, when I came back to our house, I would put myself back into my present, calling his name as I came in through the back door, profoundly grateful to hear his shout of greeting in response, and his steps, muffled by his socks or flip-flops over the wooden floor as he came to meet me in the kitchen, to hug me.

His staggering enthusiasm for me. I had only been gone 40 minutes.

One day soon after we met in 2011, long before the illness was diagnosed, he said, *You know this is it for me. If I die, I will have had you.* I wondered where he learnt to say this kind of thing. *If I die, I will have known what it is like to be loved.* From a film or a book? He had been so sure-footed, though. It felt real.

Three years later we were on a walk, this time in the country, where by then we had a house. It was November, a Saturday, early evening. The dog needed to go out. It wasn't dark, but soon would be, and we put on our coats, taking a torch as the stubbled fields surrounding our new house turned monochromatic grey and the sky purpled.

At that point, officially, the tumour was gone. There were no appointments yet in his diary to see Mr Altman, although we were aware there would be one soon, 'a follow-up', as it had been lightly referred to before the summer, as if it were for a dental appointment, or an eye test. We were walking down the concrete lane passing the semi-derelict milking parlour, descending into the valley the house lay in, with the dog already out of sight, neither of us speaking for several minutes, when he suddenly said that he found the idea of me being alive without him intolerable. I was very taken aback and took his arm. He moved on, away from me, and continued down the track. I followed, expecting him to turn around and tell me he was joking, but he did not stop and carried on, walking fast. I called his name several times but he continued up the track, the dog excitedly racing ahead of him into the copse at the top of the hill. By now we were up on the other side of the valley that faced our house, his crazed spaniel lost again in the undergrowth, sniffing around hopelessly for pheasants. The dusk was coming in fast. He stopped finally, and looked at the view back towards our house. I noticed his breathing was laboured, unusually so, but said nothing, and approached him, taking his hand, which he pulled away immediately.

What? I looked at him.

He would not look at me but said he had something else to tell me that I might not like. That he found the idea of me ever being with another man unbearable, and that although I might not want to hear this, that he wanted to strike a deal with me, a promise that I would never be involved with someone else were he to die. I looked at him and said this was completely mad and where had it all come from? Was he joking? If either of us were to die, we should both hope the other would find happiness. If I was to die, I most certainly would want him to love someone again. I tugged at his jacket, standing next to him and looking at him. He would not look at me.

Wouldn't you want the person you love to be happy? If it was me, not you... Wouldn't you want me to be happy and loved again if you weren't alive? Answer me, Andrew. You're behaving like a... I couldn't bear to use the word child, because I had such a strong sense of fear emanating from this large, powerful man. I felt his terror, but I also knew that I should not try to breach the boundary that was defending him. I waited.

He still refused to look at me and twisted the dog's lead more tightly around his wrist, and then stuck two fingers in his mouth and whistled loudly for her. I shook my head and shrugged my shoulders. I couldn't take much more of this. The dark, moist smell of the leaves was everywhere and I began to walk back down the stony path at the side of the grey wheat field. I felt estranged from him.

But suddenly he was behind me and asking me to stop. He raised his voice over the squawking of rooks from the woods: *I don't feel that way at all. I don't want you to be happy without me. I don't want you to live without me. You're asking too much. I don't ever want you to be with anyone else. Ever. You don't know what this feels like, you cannot possibly imagine having something inside you, which may kill you. You don't bloody know. I am only asking for something reasonable, which is that not everything be taken away from me.*

I shook my head and stared down the valley, whistling for the dog, listening to the rustling of some pheasants, looking at the lights blazing in our house on the other side. I thought I saw one of the boys by the kitchen window.

But you're not going to die. You're being over-dramatic. We would know if there was a problem. They would tell us.

Oh, sweetheart. Nobody knows anything. No one knows what they are talking about.

There was a profound frustration and unhappiness in his voice that I had never heard before.

We walked back separately, me leaving him to find the dog. I crossed the dark path, climbing the stile, my hands deep in my pockets, one clutching my phone. I was aware he was not keeping up with me, and when I looked around I saw he had stopped, now really searching for breath. This was not something I had ever seen before that walk, and of course I know now it was the first symptom of the cancer, alongside the backache.

A forensic recall of this brief exchange still remains. In my mind it has the quality of a 'screen memory'. A screen memory embodies an event (usually) in the patient's childhood, often insignificant but which comes back when the patient free-associates, because its meaning can only be understood much later. Like a screen memory, that conversation symbolised too much, so much that I could not bear to think about its meaning for several years, and could only recall the conversation in analysis. I realised then that this half-hour encapsulated the undoing of our coupledom. He could not bear to go, and the consequences of that, in terms of the practical chaos he left behind, would be very damaging to me and those around him.

But later I more profoundly understood his anger as

an intense envy of my ability to live and his incap-acity to do so. We never discussed it again. His words served their purpose, though, alongside a retention of and profound longing for him to be the only man I would ever love, which I believed and clung to for several years after his death. Freud talks in 'Mourning and Melancholia' of the need to prove that the 'loved object' has ceased to exist, by 'reality testing'. *Bit by bit, at great expense of time and cathectic energy, and in the meantime the existence of the lost object is psychically prolonged.* I have returned to this passionate declaration of his fury, and his love, too many times in the last five years. It angers me still that he wanted me to suffer, but I also feel now I can understand how agonising the situation was for him.

Immediately after the diagnosis and through that year, my dreams told me many stories that betrayed my conscious mind that, conjoined with Andrew's, told me everything would be fine, and we would soon be back to normal. I dreamt much more than normal, because I was repressing much more than normal. I often found myself back about to sit my finals, being handed my university examination papers. I made photographic revisits to the questions. Subject classifications returned as they never would do in consciousness. *Dante e la Media Età, Boccaccio, Ariosto e Altri Autori del Seicento, Racine, Molière et les dramaturges du 18éme siécle, Pavese, Moravia, gli Autori Moderni* – all of which I was unprepared for. I saw the typography close up on the papers, the three options, the time allowed.

And in the hazy illusory setting of the exam dream, I felt an acute shame about how poorly prepared I was. Why had I frittered away the years without revising? Freud believed almost all dreams were wish-fulfilment and these repetitive dreams were about my guilt that I could not save him, heavily disguised and incomprehensible at the time. I knew this dream was tediously common but noted how often it came. Then, of course, when I woke, there was light, there was breakfast, there were the children, and above all, there was him, fastidiously himself, and symptom-free until the late summer. It was, after all, just a bad dream.

Someone will tell us before anything bad happens, I thought. *If they can understand cancer in the way they say they do, they will tell us if he is going to die.*

12

Meetings

Psychoanalysis is both a discipline and a treatment, and I am, as well as a psychotherapist, the patient that I have been for over a decade on the couch with my analyst behind me. A full training in psychoanalysis often lasts well over ten years and rarely less than seven or eight.

The analyst sits behind the patient so they may not be seen. The patient is always lying down. They shut their eyes or maybe stare at the ceiling, wall or window. The idea is that they can free-associate more easily. Freud apparently grew tired of being looked at by patient after patient, and hence introduced the couch, drawing on Hellenic traditions of lying down to talk, relax and eat. There are many theories why lying is a more obvious posture for contemplating our interior landscapes, for talking about difficult subjects with less embarrassment or shame. Lying down is generally how we sleep, of course, inducing a loss of consciousness and allowing us to dream. So on the analytic couch, the patient is encouraged to bring that interior, unconscious world to a different kind of life in commenting on it and allowing the analyst to make interpretations.

In order to become a member of the British Psychoanalytic Society, as well as completing a complex application process, a full analysis must be undergone. This however, does not guarantee admission into the Institute of Psychoanalysis to train as an analyst. When Andrew was diagnosed with cancer, I had already been in analysis for eight years on this basis. I finally submitted my application to train at the institute in the early summer of 2014. At this point we (consciously) believed Andrew's cancer had been successfully dealt with by the radiotherapy and chemotherapy he had undergone that year.

My own analysis had changed course dramatic-ally, when Andrew was diagnosed (*as if from outer space*, as the analyst commented) in December 2013. The analyst's attempt to steer our course over the next two years did not show psychoanalysis to me at its finest. I had session after session in which I wondered what I was doing there. Every day I would arrive, lie down and say how horrendous the situation was. The analyst continued to charge me through days and weeks even when I could not attend the session as Andrew wanted me with him at radiotherapy, or a medical appointment. I knew of course that he was right to charge me (few therapists or analysts run practices without requiring their patient to commit to the session) but as I had seen with my own patients, it rankled with me. My resentment grew as the tumours did, growing worse through the summer of 2014, despite the apparent conclusion of treatment. The feeling that something awful was about to happen was often present in my sessions and interfering with my own decision about whether to apply to become a 'Candidate' at the Institute of Psychoanalysis and one day become an analyst myself.

By October, however, I felt as ready as I thought I would ever be, the analyst did not object, and the paperwork I had submitted to the institute at the end of the summer meant I was offered two interviews with senior analysts. The first one took place in a large, sparse room in Muswell Hill. There was a couch on one side of the room, and next to it, in an Ikea chair, a thoughtful-looking and very aged man who told me he would spend up to an hour and a half with me. He sat in silence once I had settled myself opposite him and waited for me to speak, his hands carefully placed flat-palmed above his knees. In due course I began to speak, explaining that I was there to discuss my application. He asked me one or two questions about my circumstances, the ages of my sons and whether I had thought about how I would manage the arduous nature of the training. I had, of course, thought about this and replied, watching the analyst's quiet frown. He gave little away as he listened. After a few more minutes of silence he asked me, quite gently, what would happen if my husband were to die before I took up my place (were I to be successful). I was both surprised and unsurprised by his directness and answered that while it would be painful, I felt I had been processing this possibility with my own analyst. As I said it, I believed it. I had another interview a couple of weeks later with a Brazilian analyst in her sixties with waist-length hair, who nodded quietly as I talked about the journey I had been on to get to this point. She smiled generously and wished me well as I left for the long drive back to my house from her dusty book-lined basement room in Acton.

Both interviewers had told me that they would not be making a decision until the Admissions Committee had met to discuss the applications in January, and although I was impatient to know whether or not I had been successful, it was enough to know that the possibility of training at the institute existed. I felt pleased that I had applied and got through the interviews. Perhaps I felt that if I was accepted it would mean I would have something to look forward to.

Two weeks later, by now late November, and after a very bad night, Andrew woke up and said he was going to request a second spinal injection for the golfing-related pain. The next day he discovered his consultant had asked for a scan.

It was as straightforward as this. The scan showed the cancer had spread.

Everywhere possible.

In desperation, I texted Wasi, who replied, *Don't worry, we will do everything we can. I am sure the results are wrong, it all seems very strange. We can save him and we will.*

The treatment we had boldly embarked on, confident of success and indeed eradication, had clearly failed completely. Mr Altman, on Harley Street, delivered the news abruptly and firmly one fresh, wet morning a day later.

I'm really sorry. It hasn't worked. Things have just not gone how we thought or hoped they would. Andrew sat silently, his fingertips touching, elbows on the arms of the now familiar chairs. Mr Altman bowed his head slightly so his kippah faced us.

If I were you, I would be on the first plane out of here. We can't help you any more. You've somehow got to get yourself to Yale. I've been talking to a colleague here; he has good contacts there. The hospital is called Smilow – it's attached to the university. It's the leading place in the world – it's the place to go for immunotherapy. I think that's the only option now. I am really sorry, but I...

Andrew stood up and clapped his hands on his thighs. He was stunned and furious.

OK, you've been clear. Thanks for that. OK. He looked at me. *Ready?*

Thanks. He offered his hand to Mr Altman. *Thanks for everything.*

As a religious Jew, this would be the first and last time Mr Altman took my hand, kindly, and slowly shook it, looking down, not at my ashen face. Andrew was already out of the room and not waiting for the lift, starting down the long staircase to get out of the building. I knew he would be angry and shocked, and that he had left me to say goodbye on our behalf. I did not know this was Andrew's last meeting with Mr Altman, but that he and I would meet again at Andrew's

Shiva, in three months' time, when he declined to come upstairs to our drawing room for the prayers being conducted.

Please come up and join the service.

No, I tend not to. It can get a bit difficult. I just wanted you to know I came to wish you long life. His handsome face was drawn and weary, as he bowed his head to me and slipped out of our front door as fast as he had come in.

So, as the year neared its end, we made our way to Yale, America, Andrew on the first flight out the next day, with one of his sons, and then me several days later, once I had squared plans for my children to be looked after by my first husband, my parents, and our long-standing childminder. I had absolutely no idea I would return without Andrew 52 days later. At that stage, incongruously, there were still so few symptoms, nothing to show other than the back pain which he still wanted to believe was related to his golf, and the slight breathlessness I had noted six weeks or so earlier, after the walk. When I had at an appropriate moment raised this and gently suggested 'a little extra oxygen' via a discreet portable tank – our kind neighbour's suggestion again – he looked at me incredulously and rolled his eyes. *Get out of here, for God's sake, woman. Are you joking?*

I was not. Nor had it escaped my attention that our neighbour's other suggestion – a second opinion – had suddenly, urgently, become the last resort.

By mid-December I was out there with him and we

were doing everything possible to get him onto the immunotherapy drug trial. And Andrew was back, the driven entrepreneur who never entertained failure. A saying of his ringing in my ear: *When I look at a deal, a five per cent chance is good enough for me, sweetheart. The odds are good.* It was the irrepressible self-belief that had got him so far, so young, and that somehow in the coming weeks would allow him to creep up his odds to 40 per cent.

Part II

This part of the book was written in the immediate after-math of Andrew's death and is set in Naples, Florida, where we had an apartment, and Yale, Connecticut, where he was accepted on to an immuno-therapy drug trial at the very end of 2014.

13

The Second Opinion

Andrew began to leave life second by second, minute by minute, hour by hour, but there was no rush, no feeling that our time together was ending. There was no sense at all that we were doing things, ordinary things, together, for the last time.

So it wasn't like the seconds before a fatal crash, a terrible fall, a bizarre accident. Nor was it like the drawn-out, exhausting closing days of a terminal illness.

This last I contemplated (a little) but I believed that in those circumstances, warnings would be issued, preparations would be made. Someone would have used the word – death, or dying. Like most aspects of our life, there would be some kind of plan in place. We were not people to be taken by surprise. So, his end, as it turned out, was not at all like one of those unimaginable and yet imaginable events that happen to other people.

I had, of course, heard some sad stories by now, at the age of 46. It did not seem that ours would be one of them. The opposite, in fact. His death was beginning however and it is not untrue to say that it was still in no way consciously anticipated.

I left London on a freezing December morning and slept through the entire flight, waking up as the plane bumped down the Eastern Seaboard towards Miami. As I sipped a bottle of water, my mouth dry and my eyes adjusting to the cabin lighting, I wondered how it had come to this. How had we ended up in America, and also why had we never thought about the full potential of this disease to beat him, rather than the other way round? Why had we left it so late to come here, when here seemed to offer his best hope? And how were we going to be here alone, without our children or any kind of support from friends or parents? His choice. It was utterly strange and I suddenly felt bereft and terrified, full of panic. As we waited to land, circling for a while over the airport, due to a delay caused by a storm up north, the man beside me turned to me and asked, *Would the plane being late inconvenience you?* I had not had a chance to take him in, having slept since take-off, but now I put down my book and said, *Not really*, and asked him the same, did he have another connection? He was a tall man, in his early sixties, with a Spanish accent. He told me he was an engineer, originally from Cuba but now living in Europe. I nodded and went back to my reading. We smiled pleasantly at each other and then rolled our eyes as the tannoy came on again and told us we would be circling now for another 40 minutes due to the congestion coming into the airport. He sighed and I grimaced.

Do you prefer to read or do you mind to talk? I

shook my head. The man introduced himself and we exchanged first names. He looked out of the window onto the haze of the city below us and then turned back to me. He explained his son had died three months before in a motorcycle crash a way up the coast. This was the first time he had been back to America since it happened. He wanted to visit the spot where the accident had taken place. His eyes welled up and he put his index finger and thumb on either side of the temple nearest me. I put my hand on his arm and said how sorry I was, and felt, for a moment, he did not even know I was there. This was perhaps my first encounter with deep grief, had I been able to recognise it outside of the consulting room. And for the first time, I found myself telling a total stranger that I was travelling to be with my husband who had stage 4 lung cancer (something I had never said aloud) as we were seeking treatment here now. The man's dark eyes looked down and he briefly placed his hand over mine, an intimate gesture. *I wish your husband the best.*

At Miami Airport, a car waited to take me over the I-75, known as Alligator Alley, an 80-mile stretch of highway fenced on both sides to prevent any wildlife creeping out onto the road from the swamps. It is straight and bleak, a bumpy-ridged concrete road with no houses or buildings of any sort. Dusk fell as the saloon car rolled along, my mobile running out of battery, my fingers tired from endlessly, pointlessly, checking Twitter, Instagram, my emails. In any case, there was no one to ring as by now both my sons would be asleep in London.

I arrived at the condominium Andrew owned in Naples, the warm air humid and humming as I got out of the car and the darkness of the gulf stretching out behind the building. I took the lift and found him upstairs, at the lift door, waiting up for me. I could see that he was slimmer than ten days before. We sat together on the sofa as I drank a glass of wine and ate the bread and cheese he had bought for me. I talked to him about the children and the extension on our house that we'd started building, until I saw him stretch himself out and wince, and I realised he was in discomfort. *Sleep, immediately,* I said, noticing as he went up the stairs that he was compensating heavily on his left-hand side. I turned out the ground floor lights and followed him up to the mezzanine where our bedroom was. I watched him take pain relief hungrily, swigging down three capsules with a bottle of water. Then we were both in bed, where we held each other, relieved to be together again as the sound of the ocean lapping on the beach came in through the huge windows. We chatted quietly about nothing, his ear next to my lips as I told him about home, and who I had seen, who had said hello, what people thought we were doing in America. I had said he had business there as I cancelled Christmas invitations we had already accepted. I knew I was also waiting for the pain medication to work, because I would not sleep until I knew his pain was under control. Within half an hour his regular breathing reassured me.

14

Beginning

*B*etween *5th January and 8th February 2015, an*
English man begins or began to die, in a condo-
minium on the Gulf of Mexico.

If this was possible. To me it sounds bizarre, and I
was there. I wrote this on 12th February, four days after
he died, and it is a line that startled me as soon as I
reread it.

Can you even begin to die? Was that why the tenses,
present and past, couldn't be settled on? Everything
gets, got, muddled. For a time I found I couldn't say
anything or think it just once; it had to be repeated to
make any sense. Or become true. *Fact, Mum.* As my
children often say. Would starting to die definitely end
in death – was that always the case? Does a person
arrive at a point when they are *going* to die, or do they
just die? Unanswerable, woodpecker thoughts.

Above the gulf, outside our apartment block, by
eight the next morning, the sun had already cruised
high. The sea a clingfilmed fuzzy blue nineteen floors
below us, the palms swooning, swaying, the occasional
car silently wending its way around the brick-paved

street of the gated estate.

Andrew lay in our bed, eyes shut, his iPad discarded on the carpet, the duvet underneath him. The sliding doors were ajar, the thin curtain blowing in and a humid breeze coming in off the ocean.

He was still and stranded. We were far from home. The reality of the situation kicked in again quickly. We weren't on holiday. Christmas had been and gone; my mother and brother had brought the children out to stay with us for two weeks, during which time Andrew had seemed himself, although I was becoming aware that he was taking pain relief more or less constantly. He was also working hard on his deal during the holiday and left me time with my mother and brother and the kids in the afternoons, not joining us on the beach. I don't think I was unduly worried over this period, or perhaps I was, and had become used to the level of dread and anxiety that every day brought. Yet there was also absolute normality externally, and no change to his routine, which disguised the reality of what was going on in his body. When he worked on a new deal, he disappeared into a vortex of intense concentrated activity which required long periods on the phone or on his computer. So I left him to it, not interrupting him and pretending things were OK.

But everyone had departed, and I too planned to go back to London to accompany the boys to settle them into the new term and sort out my own work, as it was clear to me I needed to take some time off to help Andrew. During this time, however, he was considered ready to be given the first dose of the trial drug, which would necessitate him staying at Smilow Hospital for two nights of observation. I felt very torn about not being with him for this first delivery of the drug, but we agreed that I should go back to London. We were both very unhappy about being apart but I was very worried about the children. I ended up going back for ten days, which I extended to twelve days, despite hearing a profound disappointment in his voice when I rang to explain.

OK, well, if you must. But I need you here. I really can't take much more time on my own, I seriously can't. You can sort things out later, I promise. I need you with me, love. I feel shit.

These words, still memorable and guilt inducing. He didn't sound himself, although the trial team had apparently been happy with his progress during the week following the administration of the drug.

But this time on my return, I found Andrew very changed. The first dose of the drug was already making its presence known, perhaps. There had been a noticeable deterioration during my absence which I was quite unprepared for. I wished I had not left him.

I stood in the kitchen by the tall windows and pushed the button to slowly raise the blinds. The view was of other tower blocks and in between, expansive dark-green creeks lined with sea grapes, palmettos and mahogany trees. Beyond them was the sea and its bleary horizon.

The noise of the toaster tripping the toast made me turn around. I made our breakfast, alone, which was strange. Normally every morning, wherever we were, there was an unspoken division of labour between us, him toast, me tea.

Why death came to get him (then) is still not something I understand. Over the coming months, I would be compelled to cast around urgently to understand what happened that morning.

Why did it happen? Why to him?

A sunny uplifting morning, the sea stippled turquoise velvet outside. It is not what he or I would have expected death to be like, coming to get him, here in our holiday home. Death doesn't just come to your house, to your bedroom, not now, not these days.

But this is what we do know. We are not here on vacation. The apartment is not full of his kids, my kids, friends, relatives about to arrive. We are not booking restaurants or going to the supermarket. We are here for something still shocking to me; for Andrew to go on a drug trial, to stop the cancer that is still somewhere in him, an invisible, tiny sputnik, plutonium-like in its capacity. It is impossible to conceive of. I can only try to imagine what it looks like, this psychopathic mini beast. The tumour is the size of a 'Malteser', according to the consultant – and who could be hurt by something that size? It is all so unfathomable. And yet, despite losing weight, Andrew once again looks so well – as the doctors and nurses constantly say and as he always has throughout his illness. So what does well mean when you look well but you are dying?

Until this last week. Until this pain in his back began. When I hold him in bed, one arm over his chest, I wonder why the rogue cells don't spread into me. *Who says they don't?* I wonder, crazily. If they don't know how to cure cancer then how do they know it's not contagious? If we have sex, if I swallow his saliva, might the cells spread into me? Nothing about this disease or what it is doing to him is understandable to me.

Here we are, about to go back up to New York for one last night in the city together, but we'll never go back to the Frick.

Next week we will fly up to JFK for one miserable night in a hotel on the Upper East Side, where he makes no attempt to be friendly to the doorman or the woman on reception. He knows there is no point. We arrive and we order some room service; I eat and he does not, and I then order wine and he shakes his head, fiddles around with his iPad and tells me we need to be up at 5.30am when a car will take us up to Yale where we are very much, desperately, hoping to hear that the first dose of the immunotherapy treatment has taken and that his cancer can finally be destroyed. This is the plan. We will fly between our flat in Florida and Connecticut – weekly – for him to receive the drug and he will recuperate in the warmth back by the gulf afterwards. By June of 2015 this nightmare will be over. I continuously seem to forget, however, that we are only here because the second opinion is in play, because the treatment in London, as the consultant has finally managed to tell us, has failed.

Not that it is put like that by the team here.

15

The Trial

Bluntness does not exist in the oncological team looking after Andrew that we fly up to meet, me for the first time, and Andrew for the third. Connecticut is freezing, especially after Florida's relentless sun-blasted days, and the change in light and temperature matches the change in my feelings. I feel shivery and cool, as if we too are moving into something very different. Leaving our isolated life in our flat, we will now encounter hundreds of people at Smilow Hospital, New Haven, attached to Yale University.

New York is cold but I have barely been outside, only when I left the airport terminal to go to the hotel and then again, at 6.30am, much earlier than we needed, to take the taxi up to New Haven. Andrew is, as always, keen to be early, but this seems to have developed into something more anxious and disproportionate and he has allowed four hours for a two-hour journey. I say nothing and we leave the hotel wordlessly, driving north out of the city.

I have been oblivious to the extreme weather conditions of this coastal crossroads two hours north of Manhattan until the last twenty minutes of the journey into New Haven, when the colour of the skies changes suddenly. Unlike New York, where we left a ground frost, piercing blue skies punctuating the soaring towers, here the skies are shrouded in thick cloud, muddling the horizon with the snow, which has slowed us down dramatically. Andrew starts to check his watch every three minutes and beat out a steady metronome tap on his thigh with his phone. His anxiety to be there is palpable and he starts shaking his head and screwing up his lips as the nervous driver goes slowly, anxious that his low-slung saloon will hit bumps as we turn off the highway and into the town. Andrew is next to the driver unusually. He takes a deep breath and looks out of the window. At one stage he searches for my hand, ready, on the seat behind him, and then releases his grip. Eventually, after what seems like an hour travelling past one-storey bungalows the Americans call ranch houses, mailboxes covered in snow and sparse traffic, we arrive.

We are at the hospital 45 minutes early for his appointment. The driver joins a snow-slowed queue in front of a huge, modern building, where the pavements are being cleared and several cars are waiting to drop people. We wait in turn, me touching Andrew on the wrist as he tries to get out before we have come to a stop. Pedestrians are starting to stream into the giant reception in front of us, muffled and padded against the wind-chilled air. There has, it seems, been a huge snowstorm the night before and our trainers feel inadequate as we step out of the car.

The atrium of Smilow makes me pause as we walk in through the revolving doors. It is enormous, quadruple height, with bleached-white walls and a highly lit plate-glass roof. It is a staggering piece of architecture, rather beautiful, but what strikes me most is the atmosphere, which is completely different from the empty and quiet clinics we have been in and out of in W1 for the last year.

Smilow is a cancer hospital, a type of facility we have not been to, apart from our brief visit to the Marsden. Here, suddenly, are lots of people. A jazz quartet plays by the entrance and Candy Stripers hover, kindly trying to catch a lost eye and help you to your appointment. Three people come and ask us if we need help with directions before we even get to the correct reception on the first floor. There is a long welcome desk with smiling receptionists greeting their colleagues as they arrive for the day. The air smells clean and there are giant oxygenating green plants dotted about. Several restaurants and shops are already doing brisk trade with medics in scrubs and hospital staff with lanyards nodding and smiling as they collect their coffees and pastries. It reminds me of the Richard Scarry books of my childhood that my brother and I would pore over.

It is, however, immediately obvious to me that this huge busy hospital is also full of extremely ill patients – there are literally hundreds of people here with cancer. All sorts of people – tiny children, teenagers, old people, black, white, Hispanic, thin, fat, men, women. It is, in fact, just like an average shopping mall. Except, of course, I think, they must all have cancer, or may have it, or are recovering from it. And we are here because Mr Altman, told us about this amazing new treatment called immunotherapy, which thankfully, exists now, and which in ten years' time we will accept as standard. For the unlucky third of us who will be diagnosed with cancer, immunotherapy offers the greatest possible hope for survival. Immunotherapy, we have been informed, and in the ensuing days read and googled obsessively, fights the cancer using the body's immune system rather than attacking it, as chemotherapy and radiotherapy do. This is revolutionary stuff, and Andrew, as in so much else, is an early enthusiast.

Everything is set. He feels, as do I, that he has done well, and he is pleased to be the first British patient to go to Smilow for treatment, although we also joke that this is hardly an achievement. He will be here all day until early evening, to see how the first dose of the drug is affecting him, then we will be driven back to New York for the night. I hear Andrew's name being called and see the smiling medical director of the hospital, a small frizzy-haired woman in a bright blue corporate skirt suit, waving as she descends the escalator. He has clearly already made an impact on his first two visits. *Andrew, hey!* She rushes up to him and kisses him, then takes my hand and nods with approval. *How are you? Andrew! You look amazing.* Cancer, American style, is going to be different. I feel infused with her enthusiasm as she grabs me by the shoulders and coos admiringly. *Juliet, we so all wanted to meet you, we're just so happy you're here too, we've heard so much about you. Andrew, she is as lovely as you said she was.* Andrew is responding to her and asking how her daughter is, and she chats away as we board the lift to go up to begin the battery of tests.

So we are off. The next stage has begun. Everything feels good, full of optimism. But the trial turns out to have ever increasing requirements. Once you are on the trial, certain conditions must be met. Neither of us has understood until now that staying on the trial is going to be a trial in itself.

And the further down the road we go, the more we realise it is not just a question of what we might want, but what the trial criteria are. Principally, the disease has to be serious but not too serious. As we work our way through his many appointments with people on the team, it becomes clear that over the next three weeks alone, there are some fairly major hurdles to jump. Key to continued access to the trial is that Andrew must have daily painful extractions of blood from his bruised veins to determine his white cell count.

Some people never get past this stage, because by the time they are under consideration they are too unwell and they can't get their white cell count up. It seems to relate to sufficient sleep, rest, good nutrition and vitamins, and yet also not be linked to these things. I see Andrew on form, puckering his lips and shrugging his shoulders. *No problem*. He has somehow arranged to set himself up with a local oncologist near Naples who will do the blood draws daily for him. The team nod thoughtfully as he explains his strategy, and tells them he has the best guy down in Collier County, which also means should any symptoms develop, he will be in good hands. I too listen. And I cannot stop the thoughts now, which my unconscious no longer represses or turns into guilty dreams. I am not dreaming much at all at the moment, I realise, because my real life is so strange and fantasy loaded.

After sandwiches for lunch by ourselves, we are back with an audience in a crescent around Andrew's bed. He is in a gown for the day, and I gaze at a young blonde woman, one of five medics in the room, straight out of Yale Medical School, with a Jewish surname, studious and smiling at Andrew. He has spotted her and is talking directly to her, pulling her onside, listening hard to her as she explains in patient language what the white blood cell situation indicates. I watch him nodding his head as I lose the thread and never regain it. For what overwhelms me is that this is a total lottery, which neither of us really understands.

16

Reality

The truth is that, as is his way, Andrew has boxed and bluffed his way onto the trial. I have heard him on calls with his new oncologist, a Dutch man whom he calls Hendrik. We met Hendrik once, the day after Mr Altman gave Andrew the news he could do no more.

Hendrik is neat-looking, neutral, attached to UCL and to Yale, and works from the cancer centre on Harley Street where Andrew has had his chemo-therapy. Hendrik is now the coordinator and an academic, a rising star in immunotherapy, and Andrew rings him frequently now we are in America. In the ensuing weeks, I often hear him on the phone to London telling Hendrik how he is feeling; and how perfectly suited he is to the trial. The thing is, I worry Andrew has chief-exec'd his way onto it, and I also believe he has not conveyed some important bits of information concerning his health, for example that he has Raynaud's syndrome and can't feel his fingertips once temperatures dip. *I have an auto-immune condition*, as he once told me, although now he seems to have forgotten this. His fingers go blue in the cold and he is rarely bare-footed. He had, as is his way, bulk-bought hand-warmers, little plastic packs you rip the top off which sit in your coat pockets to warm them. (I will find these for several years to come, secreted, like the kippahs and mezuzahs in unexpected places, jackets, bags, drawers.)

In other respects, apart from the tumour in his lung and the secondary tumour in his neck... *he is in perfect health.* I have heard this 50, 60 times now from him over the year, as he briefs the doctors and nurses who tend to him, take his blood, weigh him, radiotherapy him, prepare him for yet another investigation, bring him around after sedation. Yet it has not passed me by that he has not disclosed this problem with colds hands to the immunology team here in America who have come into his life to try and save it, not that that is ever said either. *Any other issues?* they ask. *Anything else we should know? Anything at all? No, no,* he says, relaxed, leading the room, two oncologists, three registrars and four medical students in a halo around his bed. He smiles at the lovely fair-headed Jewess as she goes out and shoots her a question about Yale. He's had a lot to do with a particular American university, a family connection, he tells her. *Cool,* she says, and returns to his bed, and they are away, chatting about Ivy League schools and how medicine is a total killer. Another person in his network of relationships around the hospital, from the delightful and warm director to the pretty 50-something nurse who has lost her husband to a heart attack.

Look, I've had fantastic health all my life really, I've been blessed. I lean uncomfortably against the shiny chair next to his bed and look at the nodding crescent of medics later that afternoon, a new group that has gathered. He has a bed so he can rest in between the multiple meetings and I can wait for him to be wheeled back from the many scans he has to undergo. Andrew is funny, smiling, polite, seductive. He laughs about the scanty gowns they insist he wears here, telling everyone to resist the temptation of admiring his behind. He is, as always, charming and beguiling and they are transfixed by him, by his wellness. And, I have to admit, he looks amazing, as if he has rallied. After a year of this, he's identical, super lean, tanned, strong, muscled, healthy, with not even a cough. The breathlessness is gone. There was never a cough. The back pain is brought back under control with stronger pain relief, and we return to Florida the next morning.

I feel uneasy, though. I don't feel quite truthful. I feel as if I am the junior partner not quite being straightforward with investors. I know the business is in trouble but unfortunately it is too late. I can't risk the FSA putting me on trial.

I also have so little understanding of what the doctors are trying to do (although it has been explained many times to us both in some detail) that I myself forget about his immune system complaints. I see what he is doing. He is carefully getting to a line. He has always told me that the best entrepreneurs sail close to the wind. *You just need to get to a line, sausage.* I can't say what I really think is bringing the business down. But I have a feeling of something diminishing – I cannot define it more than that.

At the same time, I know we are both very much alive today, under a sun that beats down 88 degrees of heat as I wait for him at the entrance of our condo. I have picked up our mail from the concierge and he has gone down, as he has done every one of the last six days since our return from the check-up in Yale, to the garage beneath the building. There he collects our hire car to drive up to the Sand Pine Oncology Center to get his blood taken.

I have suggested I should come too. It is a journey of some fifteen minutes, up the pale grey Naples causeway. We set off, past familiar places, the shopping mall with the Kmart we favour, the Starbucks, the Bloomingdales, the Barnes and Noble. We share a guilty love of shopping malls in America, but we don't stop today.

The sun-bleached concrete unit is an unassuming building off Tamiami Drive, identical to so many other low-rise 90s architecture in Collier County. Andrew confidently opens the door and ushers me ahead of him. To our right is a large curved reception made of mahogany, and behind it sit three middle-aged women with name badges, Kerry, Pam and Conchita, two of whom are busy with patients. The glass wall behind them is inscribed with CARE, LOVE, HUMILITY in a twisting font and has a water feature that trickles away. The room is quiet and the air conditioning a relief.

Around the large waiting room I count eleven other patients and their various carers in the company of their various stages of disease. I am quite taken aback but do not show it. It is only the third time that I have seen so many people with cancer in such a small space. I look at Andrew who is checking himself in; all three women behind reception are now looking at him and smiling. He has this way, I think.

We are told to sit down and wait.

A bloated young mother is wheeled past a few minutes later and positioned in front of us. She has a small child, maybe aged two or three, standing on the toes of her wheelchair. Her husband, thin and white despite the baking sunshine they live in, looking parched with tiredness. The toddler babbles away, seemingly unmoved by his mother's dazed features, her mouth discharging a dribble that the man wipes away every half-minute or so, without looking at her. She cannot, it seems, speak any more. I look at her, and away again.

Andrew, however, looks like Andrew. Sitting next to me, I notice and admire his size and strength. The chair is just a bit too small for him as usual. He is a tall man, just over six foot, but always seems bigger to me. His usual fine posture belies any spine pain today. He is wearing his jeans and a Lacoste shirt, loafers and his glasses. He has his iPad, which he fiddles away on. His phone comes in and out of his pocket as he checks for emails, for texts, for information on the project he is currently working on. He smiles at me, white teeth, his minty breath, his bright eyes, his smooth, brown face, a little bit of stubble today. *Do you mind, I didn't shave today?* A joke between us. *Why would I care?* I look at him and smile.

What do you give me today for my looks, though? Twelve out of ten?

I give you twenty, Andrew.

He smiles and goes back to his fidgety typing on his phone. I see from the side how fast his smile dissolves, though. He is immersed in his new business, looking up occasionally into space as he works out what to write next.

His forearms are the only real giveaway of anything at all, heavily, painfully bruised and studded with the traces of IV lines and blood draws through his darkly haired olive skin. His jeans are looser on him too; as he stands up I see how he doesn't fill them out, as he used to. He looks at me, as we hear his name, and there is both a complicity and a humility to his slight smile. I stand up too and together we are directed to the Blood Room, where he will have the first of the painful daily draws to verify 'how he is doing'. How the white cells are 'doing' (increasing) will affect how matters progress from now on. However, this process is so painful – and will become increasingly so – that he will not ask me to accompany him again.

Today I follow him. I want to see what is happening and he has agreed. A slight Mexican woman in lilac scrubs greets him warmly. *Hey there, Andrew, I can't believe you've come all the way from London to see me again.* He responds, in his flirty yet unthreatening way, *Lina, I can't believe you've come all the way from Cancun for me!* She giggles and lowers her chin to her shoulder. *You are one big flirt, señor.* I say something, joining in the banter, and she pats me on the forearm, tweaks my cheek, but I notice he doesn't smile at me. He has begun to prepare himself for what is to come.

She holds his shoulder warmly and leads him down to the suite of four large leatherette seats where they will hook him up for the blood draw. *We're just going to see how you're doing, sir,* she says first. He is weighed, another two kilos gone apparently, and his blood pressure taken, low, as normal. He makes a joke about being the only person losing weight in this, the holiday season, and the nurse smiles. *You're a fit man, Señor Rosenfeld, most certainly true!*

Yet, yet, he is clearly doing incredibly badly, or he would not be queuing up by the side of a dried-up swamp in downtown Naples to have more blood taken, every day, in order to keep him on a drug trial that requires sufferers to have reached a certain level of awfulness of the illness before they can be given the drug. It is really quite mad.

Lina then takes Andrew's arm and says, *OK, Mr R, we're going to go do the bit you don't like, but we will try and make it as good as possible, yeah?* He nods, and with a wink and a lift of his chin, indicates the direction of the waiting room where I must now return. He does not need to say he doesn't want me to see him suffer.

When his white cells reach a certain count (to us an arbitrary and incomprehensible 4000?) he will be able to have another dose of the drug. If the count isn't good enough, treatment will be delayed. There have been so many delays since 19th December 2013 by now that I am used to them.

Together in the apartment, we have now watched various films of smiling patients on the drug trial, a DVD sent by the Yale team of lung cancer sufferers talking about how well they feel, although the subtitles on the screen emphasise that *90% of the triallists do experience moderate to severe gastro-intestinal disorder within 24 hours of the administration of the drug,* and the word Pfizer floats in the left-hand corner of the screen in a delicate pale-blue script. Andrew raises his eyebrows and squeezes my hand as we watch. There is a gentle piano playing throughout these testimonies, the subjects in sharp focus in front of their sunlit sitting rooms or kitchens. I tap out a tune on his palm, watching a woman describe how good she feels, and he smiles briefly, without turning to me. This I notice. Our private joking has diminished in the last few weeks. I suddenly realise, I have not heard his laughter. How could I have missed this?

We talk a lot on the phone, as always, during these strange weeks, but in separate rooms, me to my parents, to Rachel and Jan – a doctor – and my cousins. We have got used to saying that the cancer can neither be too serious nor serious enough to get on the trial, to all of them, when they ask for clarification.

I have got into a routine whereby I get up, go for a run and then come back and make breakfast, which I take up to him, hoping he will have a mouthful of toast, or a sip of tea. His once insatiable appetite, however, has vastly diminished – and suddenly. One Friday afternoon I spend hours painstakingly making chicken soup, hoping that its smell will infiltrate our bedroom where he is sitting on the bed, working. We sit together at the dining table that night and he is so appreciative, congratulating me on the soup, and yet he maybe eats one or two spoonfuls, discreetly removing his bowl and mine at the same time so I cannot see how much remains.

The problem is that it is impossible to predict anything about this most predictable of men, and things are changing rapidly. He is still working intensely but always sitting down now – not pacing as usual, one arm supporting his elbow, the other holding the phone at his ear. He is still because to move much hurts. He works for hours as usual. The back pain, quelled by the drugs given to him at the hospital, have within two days stopped working. What I realise now is that this all happens incredibly quickly, over these four weeks. One day, I dare to say I would rather he stopped working, but he just looks at me incredulously. *Love, I'm going to be fine, you'll be happy I've done this deal one day. Jesus. Have we been told there is a major problem?*

No. We haven't. No. I shake my head. I look at him. He smiles at me.

Right. So let me get on with it.

He is much stiller than usual, but he is always on the phone, his voice booming, then quiet, questioning, reassured, typing away at his machine, his iPad, getting paperwork through and completed. But it's strange. Is it that he's a bit quieter with me? He is in some way departing by a process that I cannot put my finger on, as a son, as a brother, as a father and perhaps as a husband. He is becoming closer to himself than anyone else. This is what an illness like this does.

I am also constantly surprised by how little we both know of what is going on even at this stage. Other accounts and blogs by people with cancer I secretly read seem written in a sophisticated medical language (*My SCP was at 7 but my CFs had come down to 19, so if I make good progress the CT5 should make a real difference when I go on the Fluxotoapan. Happy days!*)

Yet Andrew and I continue to have the most tenuous understanding. Between us there are two different narratives. I err on the side of pessimism and wanting the few people who know – my parents, my cousins – to realise how grave the situation is, to compensate, perhaps, for how optimistic and breezy Andrew appears. On the other hand, when someone suggests the prognosis is anything but ultimately one of total recovery I become furious. My mother has managed to make *a sound* on one of our phone calls, perhaps with her breath, or a transatlantic phonic murmur, that suggests to me she knows he is really terribly unwell. I become very angry with her and start screaming down the line. I then feel terrible. *I'm sorry, Mum.* I ring back. *I'm sorry. I'm just in a real state.*

The fact is we don't want to know too much. For if we know too much, we are invested, captured, aware of how bad things can get. I continue my sessions with my analyst in London, by phone, when I am able. Partly this is because I have to be in analysis five times a week if I want to take up my place at the institute the following September. With the time change it is difficult, however. My analyst is silent, as usual, on the other end of the phone, but during these days, these last weeks, when we manage to hold the session, I find hearing his breathing, his odd words, comforting. I look out at the gulf, the silver-grey water curling up in a gusty wind this morning. I am up and on my phone at 5am to make my usual analysis time of 10.10 in London.

I discovered my application to the Institute of Psycho-analysis had been successful as Andrew lay dozing in bed beside me towards the end of January. Thirteen and a half months into his fourteen-month illness. An email arrived from London with an enclosure.

I was thrilled, and he, though exhausted, was typic-ally generous in his praise and happiness for me. He suggested we go to a favourite restaurant that night in Old Naples, a town near our apartment. We both knew this would be impossible, but for a few minutes we pretended it was real. We discussed what we would wear and what we would eat. He said first we were going to walk up the beach to the hotel he liked and have a glass of champagne, maybe two. Then we would walk back, fetch the car and drive to the restaurant, where he was going to have steak and chips, and a bottle of red wine. I told him I would too, although we should get a taxi if he intended to drink this much, and that afterwards we would go for ice creams at Regina's, the ice cream bar we had often been to with the children.

We managed to make a plan, a plan I knew would get no further than our bedroom, but we had a plan. A plan with all the old pleasures that had been so briskly stripped away in the last twelve months.

But, I remember that evening as one of the last happy times we had together, his pleasure at my pleasure and sense of accomplishment, my sense of achievement and expectation at the direction of my career. *I'm so proud of you. I am so happy for you. Well done. Let's celebrate.* It brought back to me our ability still to fantasise together, to be back in our old world, where our pleasures were frequent and dependable. *Why don't I go and buy whatever food and drink you want, and we can have a picnic in bed? I think going out is too much of an ask, sweetie, you're tired.* He nodded. *You're right. I am pretty shattered actually. Give me an hour to nap and I will recover.* He cupped my cheek. Smiled. Told me a joke. Then he shuffled down on the bed, and was lying next to me, an arm slung over my hips, and I remember him kissing my sweat-shirted stomach and then hearing his breathing return to unconsciousness.

This was the extent of our last celebration.

That evening I ended up silently, guiltily drinking half a bottle of wine while he dozed quietly beside me. I rang my parents, Rachel, and emailed my analyst. Unable to surf the internet any more, I found a film called *This Is Where I Leave You*, the story of a Jewish father's Shiva and the complications when all his adult children return home for it. I watched. 'Uncanny' is the word that Freud gives to those events that have inexplicable relevance often a long time after the event. I would be hosting his Shiva in under a month.

The next day, and in the few following days he and I have left together, Andrew and I do talk about the cancer, but in a rudimentary way. We blur over details, hover around the edges, squirm over the enormity of it and actually avoid speaking about it directly. I can never remember whether it is large-cell or squamous adeno-carcinoma or non-adenocarcinoma. He, the most precise and conscientious man I have ever met, certainly has no idea. Sometimes we muse vaguely over why he got it. Born with it? Stress? He didn't smoke. He doesn't overeat, drinks moderately, though he does love fish and chips. Could that be it? Or was it more complicated? Some kind of gene that went rogue? We always return to the fact of his four Russian grandparents, the men smokers and drinkers, the women, all hard workers, all who lived to their nineties, and on this note, again and again, we conclude his genes are good, and this will all work out fine. Later, much later, I think yes, it was true, we never wanted to know too much. Perhaps there was some reality after all. If we knew, we would not have been able to carry on with hope.

17

Arrival

But... death. Here it is. Suddenly. One day. It is in our huge American bed, it is under our duvet, settling in, downy and comfortable. Spreading itself around. Deciding. Meanwhile, as the sea wind blows in the voile at the terrace doors, Andrew stretches minutely, breathes in deeply and frowns, realigning his long, straight spine and turning slowly onto his side. His jaw clenches. The muscles of his dutifully worked-out trunk cushion around the bones, but the pain wakes him. Whatever they have given him at Smilow is not working.

The bellow of pain through his bones is so agonising that he remains completely still, winded by the splice of nerve, muscle and cartilage that comes like a gunshot into his body. He keeps his eyes shut, as he now knows it is best not to open them until this subsides.

All this takes place in silence. No one watches, and this is how he prefers it. But I know it is what is going on in the bedroom above me.

No, I thought, as I watched the kettle and buttered

my toast. No, we would be told, before it even comes close to that. Death comes planned, and plenty of warning is given. As I think this I am aware how transgressive it feels to allow the possibility of death into these conscious thoughts. It is not allowed because the person I am thinking about is still alive. That is the point, and he could not bear me thinking about him as a dead man. It would be unforgivable of me, and therefore, I may not do it. I cannot stop it now, though. The apartment, bought during his long first marriage, has become full of a different atmosphere for me. I do not feel at home, as I once did. My fervour to fill the glossy empty kitchen with food and ingredients is waning. My jars of spices and organic condiments promising many health-giving properties will not be used. A new recipe book sits squarely on the huge island. *The Anti-Cancer Diet*, next to *What To Eat If You Have Cancer*. There are others too. Andrew has not even noticed them. Beside them is the juicer, another one, bought to make the terrible frothing broths of vegetables that he has loathed from the start. Next to this are plastic sachets and tubs of maca, chia, turmeric, ground linseed, all the nonsensical stuff I am trying to get into his body. We both know it is totally pointless but, like a dog with a bone, I persist.

I retrieve two plates from the dishwasher, take the tray from above the fridge. We are not near that point in any case, for there has been no mention of him dying. I reach for the Marmite, smuggled from London. The kettle's urgent noise fills the whole kitchen suddenly and

I hope he will not be woken by it.

I still do not say it, let alone refer to it; no one says *that word*, or its variants. And it has simply never been spoken of by the doctors. It is almost an outrage that anyone would say it. I fear for whoever says it first in front of him. It may be me. Or it may not.

So we never discuss death. All the hope, the wishful thinking, his control, his dictates, the minimising, the fighting talk, the *I am different*, the authority he has elsewhere will all be proved hot air. I have listened since the beginning, thirteen months ago, to his explanations of the progression of the disease, to a doctor, to those who know, wincing at his invention and spin. I have had to leave the room on more than one occasion to stop myself from cutting him off, taking away the phone. It embarrasses me to hear him, playing down the sickening, terrifying reality. I feel there will be consequences somehow.

That I even have these angry thoughts makes me feel guilty and wretched. I cannot tolerate, as I can other conflicting feelings about many other subjects, my anger with him, fear for him and need for him all at the same time. I split off the first two. Eight years of psychoanalysis, ten years of treating many patients, but my tolerance for ambivalence eludes me when it comes to him. The intense wish that he will survive this thing overcomes me. Deep in my unconscious is an equally fervent belief that there is no battle or struggle or recovery from an enemy that had defeated him before we were even aware of its presence.

Moreover, I can't say any of this to anyone, least of all to him, because to do so would be heresy, betrayal – to say nothing of sadistic. And yet, today in America, in this vast state where we are two tiny people at the top of a tower block, something is beginning to happen; his body is preparing to inhabit a different place. More precisely, his body is starting to stop working and his mind, his thinking, is in retreat, a necessary narcissism, a closing of the shutters. With illness, the mind turns in on itself, to prevent an overextension of energy anywhere but where it is needed to mount a defence against attack. This, but in a giant, final way, is what is happening.

I put the toast onto the tray with two mugs of tea, his with the bag still in, mine weaker with a scant half-teaspoon of sugar that I deny him. I cross the hall and start up the staircase to the bedroom and push open the door of our room. The sun catches the stone of the stairs and my brown feet pad over the carpet. It is going to be 89 degrees today. The other four condos stretching in a neat line up the coast are plastered in that pale-butter Floridian yellow, looming twenty floors up, edging the Gulf and seeming to pop out of the dark green Everglades tangle that stretches south for miles. The sea is calm, and I see the tractors raking the sand down by the water. Couples older than us power-walk up the beach, often hand in hand, sometimes with oxygen tanks, sometimes with small dogs.

We've not made it down to the beach for a while now, I think.

Andrew. I've made tea, breakfast. There is a short silence. His back is to me.

Great. Thank you.

Quieter, not him, not his familiar, low, accent-less voice. This is whispered.

Withdrawn. Not asleep. I can hear where he is by his breathing. I put the tray down on a low table. By the sofa that no one sits on in our bedroom. Until now. It is where I sit. And watch. He is curled, his brow vexed. Eyes shut. Sleep. Of a sort. He has not been on the phone the last couple of days. He is starting to slip away. Somewhere away from me. I don't know how I know this, why I feel it, but I do. The tiredness, which he has complained of since I got back, is now becoming chronic. A feeling, he says, of utter exhaustion; he has never known anything like it. I have been telling him this is normal and what does he expect? He has never stopped, throughout this whole time he has kept going, submitted to the treatment, the chemo, the radio, now this immunotherapy trial. But he has never stopped to be ill. To rest. He needs to rest to get better. I tell him this all the time but I do not believe it. On top of this he says the malingering back pain is now starting to nag at him in a different way.

It becomes what we talk about.

All we talk about.

Over the last few weeks, since just before Christmas, cardboard pharma boxes have been clustering by his side of the bed. I see they are stockpiled, which is very him. And yet not.

Any attempt to tidy the boxes makes him angry.

Please don't touch them. Please. Don't touch them. I know where everything is. Listen to me. Please.

He says this from under the sheet where he lies very still on his side.

I have no idea yet of how obsessive this need to control the last piece of the world he can control will become. I will see it in his last days in hospital, 25 days from now. I am not easily deterred, though.

I just want to make it easier for you.

I've asked you. No. Just don't touch it. Please.

I obey and step back, feeling thwarted and a little humiliated. The neat white cartons with primary, coloured sections and lettering tower over his *Middlemarch* and *New Yorker*.

I want to read about what he is taking.

He has never, to my knowledge, believed in or bought painkillers. He wouldn't even know where to find my Nurofen. For the last two weeks, however, beginning with Advil and Motrin, taken irregularly at first, then every four hours, he has been developing a habit. These are what he refers to as *OTC* (Over The Counter) remedies in a call with the trial nurse to check in on how he is doing before our next visit to Connecticut. I hear him discussing how they are not relieving the pain. This is a change. An admission of something.

I am sure it's nothing, I know it, just the old golfing pain. My body is still more sensitive, I guess, but, I do need something stronger. It's got nothing to do with the cancer, I assure you. We definitely need to sort this out.

I hear a muffled voice on the other end.

Yeah. OK. Is there nothing we can do from here? Can someone not give me something stronger? The call ends shortly and I continue to listen at the door of the bedroom.

A strong but weary breathing starts again.

18

Preparation

On 21st January we fly, leaving Fort Myers at sunrise, heading directly up to New Haven for Andrew's last visit before the next dose of the drug. Andrew is quiet and preoccupied as we quickly begin the cruise over the vast swamps, crossing over Tampa, then Miami, up past Jacksonville and towards South Carolina. The flight is smooth, and the cabin fills with dazzling light from the east as we skim the coast. I want to engage him in hopeful conversation about the day, and tell him how well he has done and how happy I am he will soon be given a second dose of the drug but he becomes more withdrawn the more I say. We hold hands across the narrow aisle and he lifts his chin and nods to me, blowing me a kiss before looking down at his phone, where he is typing a long email to be sent when we land. The blinding sunshine gives way swiftly to cloud and soon we are bumping down-wards. I see dark-grey clapperboarded houses on the peninsulas that spike out into the freezing Atlantic, as we descend sharply and slide into a landing on the compact airfield, the snow frothing up from both sets of wheels. New Haven is knee- if not thigh-deep in snow, we have our huge parkas, scarves and gloves with us, and I truss Andrew up as we ready ourselves to get off the plane, tying his long scarf twice around his neck. *Get off me, woman,* he smiles. He moves past me, and I see him bend his legs uncertainly as he descends the short steps onto the runway. He takes a deep breath and looks anxiously for the Uber, which is waiting by the small airport building.

In fifteen minutes we arrive at the hospital, and the director, rushes towards us, hugging Andrew, who warmly responds, and then me. She hands him a piece of paper with his itinerary for the day and clutches his arm, leading him up the escalator from the sunlit stone court full of shops. Brahms is being played today by an elderly pianist, her pages being eagerly turned by a young Chinese man. It is early but a couple watch, a middle-aged woman on crutches, her elbow held by her companion. There is brief light applause from around the huge space as the woman draws to a close and prepares for her next performance. I am happy to be back there.

When the second dose is given, two weeks later, on 2nd February, Professor Saul Cohen, a large smiling man with curly grey hair, sharp eyes and a slightly lispy Brooklyn accent, will be in charge. He is both a consultant and an academic with a chair here at Yale and at UCL in London. He is softly spoken, deliberately thoughtful, Jewish, exactly Andrew's age, and Andrew likes him. An understatement. As with Mr Altman there is a deep respect. Today we are here for the obligatory check-in with the hospital that the Drug Company, as it is always referred to, insists upon, so we won't see him, which I can tell Andrew is a little disappointed about.

First, though, we are dealing with other matters, what the nurse describes as a 'housekeeping visit', as we take the massive lift up to the tenth floor. The first issue to be dealt with is the back pain. We find we are booked in with a consultant from a different discipline, one we have never had any dealings with – a rheumatologist – and I feel indescribably happy. For the first time in weeks, I feel we are being whisked thrillingly into normal, non-terrifying, non-cancerous medical space. Nothing bad can happen in rheumatology, I think. Andrew has the appointment because he has admitted for the first time, properly, to this pain in his back. I heard him on the phone the day before to the nurse. His breezy excitement was gone: *It's total agony, I've never known anything like it. I am really desperate. Nothing is working. You need to hit me with something very very strong.* It is a big moment, although he does not know I have overheard him. He has told me many times of the strength of this pain, but never anyone else. So there has been some honesty. It is the first time in thirteen months that Andrew has admitted that something is not going to plan.

We are put in a little room on the ninth floor, in one of the twin towers of Smilow Hospital, and here, a few minutes later, is the rheumatologist, from that most docile of medical disciplines. This doctor is a tall, slight man, with an Italian surname, olive-brown skin even in the cold Connecticut winter and big tortoiseshell glasses. He tells Andrew that it's most likely, as is often the case with former sportsmen, that it's his lifetime of swings that's giving him trouble. He's done some homework on this big Englishman in front of him.

Andrew nods approvingly.

He listens carefully to Andrew explaining the problem. Then he hears about the symptoms and finally nods as Andrew gives him his diagnosis. The pain relates to his historical slipped disc. Does the doctor understand?

Without missing a beat, the doctor nods and says that there is a clear solution, which is called targeted pain relief. They can move him into a different zone of pain solution now, to really kick the pain right out of touch. He describes several options – naproxen, Aleve and the surely sarcastically named Celebrex.

Andrew reiterates that his slipped disc is playing up, and smiles, but the young doctor now becomes firmer.

It doesn't really matter where the pain is from, sir, the point is getting way ahead of the pain. You need to always be on top of it, so it never overtakes you. Make sense?

Andrew frowns and then asks about side effects, which the doctor says will wear off, although he concedes there may be a few. Andrew asks what this means and is told he may feel a little sleepy, a little out of it, some digestive issues. He rolls his eyes, frowns again and I can see he is about to ask whether there is anything he can take with no side effects, when the doctor politely steps in.

If I may, sir, in America you would be called a narcotics-naive patient, and you need to get ahead of the pain. I can't say it plainer. He smiles warmly and looks at a thick book, flicking through to a page and then scrolling down Andrew's notes, all in front of him on a centralised and highly efficient hospital system. *Is that me?*

Y'sir. I got it all here. I was just thinking about how much we could put you up to. That's a pretty healthy solid weight, which is going to work in our favour. He is intently typing, his finger on the book of drugs, turning now to another page. Andrew smiles a little at this point and looks at me. *Totally right, narcotics naive. I never need to take anything. My wife takes more than me.* I grin at him. *I just never have anything wrong with me.*

The doctor smiles at us both and I see him look quickly at his watch. This is good news, we're going to be out of here in a few minutes.

He says they will give him something that should be super-effective. He warns it may take a little while, but just a couple of days and life is going to feel a lot easier. When Andrew finishes the immunotherapy treatment, they will review him.

Say in a year to 18 months. He will stay in touch with the trial team, of course.

The two of us smile suddenly when he says this. Andrew grabs my hand into his lap under the desk between us and the doctor. Any talk of being on the other side of this is welcome, incredible. Anything long term, anything that you have to take for the rest of your life, anything chronic, is just lovely. The doctor stands up smartly, and Andrew eases himself to his feet, dismissing my offer of an arm. But he is clearly in pain again.

Thanks. Thanks so much.

You too, sir. Heard about you from my colleagues and a pleasure to meet you.

Please, call me Andrew.

Andrew. Yes. I heard a lot about you from the trial team, actually. You've come a long way. They're doing a lot of good work in London, I hear. It's UCL right? I always wanna say UCLA. We smile again. *Oh, I'm sorry, I forgot – I should say now that I am gonna be handing you over to Palliative, as those guys –*

Palliative, did you say?

The atmosphere changes all at once. Andrew tilts his chin slightly, his head to the side. The smile is still there but cold. The doctor notices, and carries on.

Oh, sure, sure, but absolutely no need to be alarmed, sir, Andrew. Sorry. Over here Palliative is the pain relief guys, it's the same thing. Basically, a background in anaesthetics. The guys everyone wants to know, right? Ignore the word palliative in this context, totally. I mean they work with the end-of-life end of things but we're not talking about that here.

Andrew's smile returns. *Good, glad to hear it.* He nods, as if the doctor has passed a test.

Well done. Good man. Good to meet you, Andrew

is saying, shaking the doctor's hand. *Really appreciate you helping me, just amazing, what an amazing hospital this is.* He puts another hand over the doctor's delicate wrist. A powerful businessman smile. I have seen it many times before. It is somehow strange here in this tiny cubicle of a room. Out of place, but I can't put my finger on why.

That day there are more tests to be done before we will be allowed to return to Florida, where the two-week wait for the next dose of the drug trial will begin. I sit in the corridor while Andrew is taken up and down, looked after, all over the hospital. I see such interest and warmth from the nurses in their scrubs, sometimes patterned with Mickey Mouses, or pale pink, or flowered, and their brightly coloured Crocs. He seems to know all their names and as he is brought back to me in between scans and blood, urine, and other tests of every possible kind. I am introduced to them all, and told how lucky I am to be married to this incredible guy, as he is complimented on his lovely wife. I am moved, as always, by his great capacity for getting people on side, getting them to help him. He told me once, soon after we met, that as a young man, starting out in business, he had nothing, so he had to somehow find something to give people in exchange. He gave, I see now, of himself, and it is this, and a sincere interest in the other, that wins him help and admiration. Here are Ellen and Marsha, two oncology nurses whose stories he knows already, and whose children's names he tells me as they come to take his blood pressure yet again. He is treated so kindly, and I begin to feel some returning sense of confidence that this is all going to be over soon and we may actually, one day, be going back to normal.

Eventually, at seven that evening, we leave the suffocating heat of Smilow. The relentlessly kind director, who has sat with me for several long chunks of the day, chatting about her visits to London and her Italian grandmother, comes down to the giant cathedral-ceilinged reception to wave us off. She hugs him passionately. Andrew's capacity to charm people both pleases and unnerves me.

Yet he is quiet and withdrawn as we are driven back to the small airstrip outside New Haven. The snow lies deep on both sides of the road, which is gritty and slow. We are in a Mercedes saloon with an Uber driver who is wrapped up in an overcoat and wearing a baker cap. There is no sound apart from the soft crunching of snow under the tyres.

Andrew looks down as soon as we are moving. I see his head drop a couple of times and lift up again. His nose is so straight and I find myself thinking, *How do you have such a beautiful straight nose?* I feel a rush of desire and warmth, and pleasure that he is out of the hospital and we are alone again, in charge again.

I put my hand on his knee but he does not reciprocate. His neck is bent.

Don't. Please. Please, love. I just need some space.

I feel tears puncture my eyeballs. His voice is sharp, blunt. I know it is the pain causing this, but I too bruise easily.

Please don't touch me.

He has never, ever, pushed me away, turned me down.

I retract my hand. Memories of an ancient relationship in my twenties with a sadist come back again; pathetic reaching out to meet rejection, then desire, then drawing in, then out again. The more he said no, the more I begged. Ultimately, I didn't want him, which was, as is the way of the sadomasochist, when he decided he wanted me. I learnt a lot.

Still, I shudder, feeling miles away from Andrew. I can't have thought about this man for years. The thoughts disturb me. I remember Andrew's fury years back when I told him about this man as we both began the slow unveiling of previous relationships, inevitable as a new couple starts out.

In good health, Andrew was a very strong man, and a man who knew how to process his anger, to safely expel it. Now his anger has nowhere to go, no discharge. I feel his anxiety about me, though at the moment, he cannot express it. What will happen to me if he is not there to protect me? Is this on his mind? Or just mine? Exhausted, his head now hangs as we bump down the snow-quietened roads to the airstrip. Before we left, the hospital dosed him up intravenously, and with two tramadols, which he took with a plastic beaker of water, looking at the nurse as he did so. Those brown, watchful eyes. *It might make you a little out of it, sir, but we wanna get you back down to Naples comfortably.* He is looking down at his lap. His big, powerful thighs, hard, square, reassuring blocks, yet the selvage of the denim does not encase his legs as usual. There is a little space now, on either side. His hands are clasped loosely between them. His fingers are looking softer, frail even. He too is feeling completely and utterly alone, this much I do know. He is in that place where I am not tonight. He is there alone just now, in The Room Next Door.

19

Flight

The fiercely cold Connecticut January night is as oppressive as the hospital heat we have left. We wait for ten minutes or so in what passes for a terminal, a small beige lounge with strip lighting in a PortaKabin on a landing strip. Paperwork and technical checks on the little jet that will take us back down to Florida are being done. I sign all the documentation, while Andrew sits down again, his head dangerously near his knees.

We have cancelled our commercial flights because Andrew cannot sit in a car for two hours back to Newark airport. From now on, Andrew has decided we will charter planes to get back and forth from Florida.

I have not argued with him about this, although it goes against the way I feel we should live. On the other hand, the idea of sitting on a Jet Blue flight from Newark down to Fort Myers seems suddenly impossible. I don't actually know how he would even queue in an airport.

He is clearly exhausted by the day and – with a few moments of honesty – by still trying to prove to the team he is not really ill. For twenty minutes we sit, as the aircraft is checked, hearing occasional bursts from the receptionist's headphones. The local TV station news comes on, warning of a very bad front moving in from the Atlantic tonight. There is, it seems, as the next half-hour unfolds, some anxiety about the weather. Two men come in from the runway, and the pilot follows. They disappear into a room off the lounge. It is getting late, but there is a choice to be made. We continue to wait, but at a certain point Andrew sits up sharply. *Fuck*. He straightens up. *Fuck*.

OK? I ask.

No, not OK. What's happening? It's 7.30. We need to be out of here. You can't fly past eight. What's going on?

Just then, the pilot appears and tells us that although they are satisfied it is perfectly safe to fly it is going to be a bumpy ride. A huge storm has blown in over New Jersey and will bring with it a bit of a chop on the route down. However, they will try and level it out as much as possible for us. The pilot is big bellied, moustachioed with a comical captain's cap on and short sleeves in the iced night. Andrew is looking more exhausted than I have ever seen him. He nods and says we are ready to leave. The co-pilot, a small Latino man with warm eyes, smiles at me and offers to carry both our small cases to the aircraft. He opens the door, ushering in freezing air. I adjust the scarf wound tightly around my neck and check the zip on my parka. I want to tuck Andrew's scarf in but I don't think he wants me near him. He stands, very slowly, shaking his head from side to side.

The aircraft is a black outline on the tarmac, maybe 25 metres away. With my head thrust down into my scarf and my parka hood up, I begin to walk towards it but hear my name and see Andrew looking forlornly at the distance.

Can you bring a car round? I'm not going to make it.
No problem, sir.

It is an absurdly short journey but I go back the twenty or so steps I have just taken for I know I must sit next to him, so as not to humiliate him further. He is helped into the car that belongs to someone in the airport, then sits next to me, his eyes shut. He winches himself up the short stairs onto the plane, where he declines both the seats pointed out to him and immediately lies down on the thin mustard-coloured sofa at the back of the tiny cabin. He does not speak to me and shuts his eyes, his lids now thin and veiny, I notice.

The pilot leaves us to it, seeing that Andrew wants no help and I have merely smiled at him politely, not engaging in chat about the weather, journey or timings. He and the co-pilot begin their checks, laughing about a baseball result.

I can't say a word and it is as if Andrew's psychic and actual anorexia, his nil by mouth, is starving us both now. The pain relief must be kicking in, and he is already disappearing into a deep pharmacological sleep. I belt him in, sliding the clasp under his hip as he winces, and then put a blanket over him. *It's all right sweetie, it's all right.* I say this to him tonight, as I would to one of my sons. He is being dragged away by something, I feel it so keenly. Now he would be pulling me down with him, his arms around my neck, wanting me next to him, making a joke about wanting to make love to me on a plane. I wish I could hold him in my arms and rock him, this six-foot man, slipping away in front of me.

I'm shattered, Juliet, I am shattered I…

His voice is flagging; he can barely speak. I hush him and place my scarf carefully under his head, seeing his brow corrugate as he is touched again. He wants oblivion, and to be left alone.

The co-pilot asks me if he needs to give us safety instructions and I shake my head. *No, no, we're fine.* We taxi rapidly down the runway, the lights around the airfield blinking red to guide our take-off. A steady, determined acceleration and we are sharply up. New Haven is soon below us, now an icy ink blur as we begin to head out away from the coast. Few lights are on, and I realise many of the houses must be holiday homes. The sense of emptiness is compounded somehow by this. I can't wait to leave, although I am worried about Andrew, and whether he should be this far from the hospital, whether we should even be leaving. I have a bad feeling. He whimpers as the plane hurtles up into the black air and I look back but his eyes are shut. He is soon out completely; the tramadol has finally kicked the pain into touch.

He does not move again, even as over Georgia I catch my breath when the plane suddenly flips up and then down several times. The storm that has doggedly followed our flightpath down the coast appears to be catching us up. We were warned about this, and I am not a nervous flyer, but even so, it doesn't feel good. Another huge jolt upwards, then we are falling down again. I feel my empty stomach viscerally now. I have eaten so little in the last few days.

Now, as a rattling sound begins at the back of the plane, I wish I had a drink in my hand, but as with food, I haven't had the heart for a glass of wine in the past few weeks either, and there is none on board.

I do, however, still have books.

I read, have always read, and now, these days, while I wait for Andrew, here and there, and while he sleeps, I have had more time to read than I have had since I was a student. Rachel is my friend of 30 years, and a writer. She emails me suggestions of what I should read next, and I have been burning through them.

Rachel has counselled against me reading one particular book now, although she recommended it a couple of weeks ago. Amazon has delivered it in the meantime. *Levels of Life* by Julian Barnes. She is not sure it is suitable for me, just now, and I have not asked her why. However, because I am running out of suitable reads, the book is in the bottom of the bag I took up to Yale, and I started it this afternoon as we waited to be discharged. I am towards the end of the short book, high up in the air, being pushed around by strong winds above North Carolina, when I realise (rather late) that the book is about the death of his wife.

You put together two people who had not been

together before... Then at some point, sooner or later, for this reason or that, one of them is taken away. And what is taken away is greater than the sum of what was there. This may not be mathema-tically possible, but it is emotionally possible.

As the book ends, I begin to realise that it is all about an atrocious grief, the loss the author can only imagine that he sustained because he has not killed himself.

How strange, I will think three years later, *that I did not know I was reading about someone losing their lover. That I did not think that I was in the same situation, or would be shortly.*

It does not cross my mind. Instead, I find myself staring blankly out of the window into black battering rams of rain on the short wings of the Lear jet. The aircraft is now shaking violently and I realise how scared I am.

The pilot and co-pilot are talking, their headphones on, and I hear the odd *Sure! Go right ahead,* then *Pull, pull, pull, who-ah baby, that was a big one, Lordy!* I look back at Andrew for reassurance as the rollercoaster begins to swell through the vapour. The engine is rendered alarmingly inaudible by the rain attacking the aircraft with a massive drumming. Has it stopped? The shaking suddenly tosses my bottle of water to the floor and I look back again to Andrew, but he is unconscious, his brow still furrowed. The cabin is a tiny rattling coffin and Jesus Christ, I am not scared of flying but I would, just now, have wanted his warm hand. He would have smiled.

Sausage. Oh my sausage. You're not scared. (A wink.)
I love it. I love a bit of turbo-charged turbulence. Then
back to his book, his furious reading. His hand across
the narrow aisle on my thigh, or his feet between my
thighs opposite him. *Take those things away from me.*
Him pushing the vast box of Krispy Kremes the aircraft
contractor supplies for these flights.

Don't let me. It will ruin my figure. You are trying to
ruin my figure. You're a feeder, I get it. I still love you.
His smile at our great good fortune. *How lucky we are,*
my love, to have found each other. How very lucky.
Would you rub my feet?

These banal silly conversations, the language of the
intimately committed, still come to me. A lot of swearing.
Smiles and his hands cupping my face, my chin. I can
see and feel his white teeth, his face, those large topaz-
brown eyes with a slow blink. A little rub of his eyes
while he rests his glasses on top of his head. A little silk
square out of their case and now he is cleaning them
intently. Then settled again on his fine nose. The exact
way he would clean his glasses. Rarely now, however,
can I hear the sound of his voice.

For now I watch him, bent, deeply asleep, his huge
parka still on, covered with the blanket. He is lost to me.
His absolute silence is a counterpoint to the increasingly
harsh percussion of the storm on the plane. The curtain
between the cabin and cockpit swings rapidly like a
metronome as the body of the aircraft rocks through the
storm. I feel sweat collecting on my upper lip and scalp
as I see the pilot's huge hairy forearms pulling back hard

on the yoke. He still chats to the co-pilot, and I hear an abrupt burst of laughter, but I sense a difference now in their tone. There is an intense concentration between them and at one point the co-pilot energetically wipes down the inside of the windscreen with a cloth. There are several violent jolts, which cause me to grab both arm rests, while looking back for Andrew. I need him to tell me we will land safely and that it is all fine and what are we going to have for breakfast when we get back to Naples.

The plane now seems to be flying through a theme park, on a giant gravity ride, the kind of place my sons dream of being taken when they are older. The co-pilot looks back at me with a weak smile and a thumbs-up, while he continues to wipe down the window with a little cloth. Then down we go again, a steep awful pitch this time, the lights below seemingly closer, the ocean to our left black and accommodating. *Shit*. The book slips in my damp palms.

I look down and try to lose myself in it again while wondering if I should get up and just lie down next to him on the narrow couch, but there is insufficient space for two people. If we are going to die, let me be next to him. Then I realise – aha! I am finally being compelled to look at death, my own as well as his, and he is not going to die of cancer at all, no, he is going to die in a plane crash, with me next to him or on top of him. Our bodies will be washed up on some beach south of Tampa, the wreckage found as far away as Key West and the Bay of Biscayne, the pilot and co-pilot gone to a watery grave too. Christ, *shut up*. My rational mind is back. Statistically, I say to myself, breathe, stop being such a narcissist. *Stop it.* ... I determinedly open the book again.

We live on the flat, on the level and yet – and so – we aspire. Groundlings we can sometimes reach as far as the gods. Some soar with art, others with religion; most with love. But when we soar, we can also crash. There are few soft landings. We may find ourselves bouncing across the ground with leg fracturing force, dragged towards some foreign railway line. Every love story is a potential grief story. If not at first, then later. If not for one then for the other, Sometimes, for both.

As we judder through the night, and the plane gradually begins to glide smoothly again on the gentler air pockets as we near the warm south, I feel no relief. The divination games I played with myself are still in my mind, we crash, you survive, he dies of cancer, you get it later, you both die, the plane crashes you die, he recovers, the children, the children, the children. I feel like I am going mad with the uncertainty and terror his illness has brought. And also not going mad at all. *Every love story is a potential grief story.*

The flight softened, I stopped thinking I was going to die, but we were never out of troubled little air pockets, sliding this way and that, up and down on the chutes of January wind until suddenly, over Tallahassee it levelled out, and down over Tampa the light changed to the darkness of the southern-hemisphere summer.

20

The Beach

The plane landed quietly at Naples and I do not recall at all the journey back to the apartment. He could barely speak, for what reason, exhaustion, pain, I did not know. He would not let me help him and I went to bed, casting off my clothes and pulling on a T-shirt. I brushed my teeth and fell asleep almost as my body touched the sheet. I woke at 8.40 and wondered guiltily how he had come to be next to me, his night uniform of shorts and a T-shirt on. How much effort it must have taken him to change.

I have wondered whether it was a dream, but on 26th of January, we managed one last visit to the beach. For some reason he was feeling a little better. Dying, I now understand, like most things is not linear. He had rallied, perhaps, as we had momentarily, finally, got the dose of pain relief right.

I'd like to go to the beach today. Lie about for a bit, then go to the club for lunch. What do you say?

He looked at me and gestured to the huge expanse of water shimmering through the gauzy curtains of our bedroom windows. I tapped the bottles of pills next to him and pointed to the glass of water I had brought up.

I say OK. I say let's go, sweetheart. I'll get my costume.

The condominium he had bought fourteen years before he met me was set 150 metres back from the sand, in a gated community with a long paved road running through carefully manicured gardens on either side. A three-minute walk at most and one we had done numerous times with the kids, with spades, bags and balls. That morning he dressed, slowly, while I gathered our usual bag of beach stuff. He came awkwardly down the stairs, gaunt but handsome, dressed for the first time for several days, in a polo shirt and shorts. As we took the lift down to the building's reception he frowned.

You need to go down to get the car, please, he announced as I pushed the glass door out into the baking humidity, holding it open for him. He looked, anxiously, up at the sky.

Sorry, darling. That sounded sharp. Sorry. I just mean, you need to do the car today, I can't and... and like – now. He raised his voice suddenly and gripped the low wall bordering the entrance. I took a deep breath and tugged gently at his shirt, cupping his cheek and turning his face towards me.

Andrew. Love. I'm really not sure we should actually leave home today, you know. This is a bad idea. You've done well getting down here but let's just go straight up again, shall we? It's not even sunny at the beach. Wind's up. I gestured to the beachgrass shaking in the grey sand metres away.

No. We're going. He took a breath with some discomfort. *We're going. Get the car, love.*

I left him, propped up by the large mock-Italianate stone archway and ran down to the garage beneath the condo, everything taking for ever, the shutters on the garage, the garage doors where the car was, reversing the giant SUV out, not caring whether I hit a concrete pillar or not. My heart began to race, then I was moving, too fast, through the empty car park, up the ramp and back out into the light, swinging round to the wall. He did not look up at me, and I jumped down from the stupidly high seat to go and help him.

OK, still wanting to go? My voice was uncertain, hollow.

No, love, leave me, it's fine. He limped around to the passenger side, patting the vehicle. He winced as he heaved himself up into the car's dark interior.

Jesus, Jesus. Fuck. He was staring forwards, gripping the seat. *What the hell is going on?*

I looked at him and put my hand on his arm. He smiled fast, still looking straight ahead, not at me. Then his jaw relaxed again.

You're just getting used to moving again. Don't worry. Let's take it slowly, Andrew. My mouth dried.

S'OK. Let's go. He winced. *Ah. Fuck. Oh God.* His eyes were tightly shut.

Andrew... Should we call this a day? Leave it. I think we should? I bit my lower lip.

No, he said, he wanted to go to the beach.

Let's go, Juliet, now. I want to go to the beach.

I drove down the tiled road, in under a minute, passing the three other condos that lined the street to park behind the bike shelters. The sky this morning was low, oppressive, some rain forecast. Without turning my head, I looked at him, wondering how he would get out of the car. He stared down at his lap. I got out of the car and ran round to the other side, as he opened the door.

I'm fine. It's OK, leave me, please. But I took his bag, as always full of his papers, iPad, and books, and hoisted it to my shoulder. And he didn't argue.

The boardwalk, dyed a dull silver by the relentless wind and buffeting sand, stretched out ahead of us. I took his hand as we walked. He limped the ten metres or so, grimacing with each step. I looked away, knowing that anything I could say could make it worse.

Eventually we were at the sand, which made it harder. He found himself barely able to stand and looked around for something to hold onto. I grabbed him.

The lone deckchair guy on duty came up to him, jogging neatly over from his hut where he kept the parasols and chairs. A familiar face Andrew had known for years. No one was on the beach today.

You all good there, Mr R, sir? Been more'na few weeks we didn't see you out here. We missed you, sir! He rubbed his hand and reached for Andrew's. They shook hands, Andrew clasping the man's hand with both of his own.

Put your umbrella and chairs out, sir?

Sure, yes, thanks, Diego, I got a bad back, kept me

inside. He handed him $20. *We won't stay long; it's not the weather for it.*

No, sir, this has to blow over soon, sir, you can't be out here for one day and not get the Naples sunshine, sir. Law against it!

It surely must. Andrew smiles, but I see he is looking unsteady.

This afternoon saying it's gonna be fine.

He arranged two deckchairs, two low armchairs and a cabana for us. I looked at him as he gestured to me to sit down.

Just let me do it, don't help me, I just need to...

Eventually we were both sitting, in the low armchairs, the blowing sand pricking my calves.

After less than twenty minutes, Andrew said he needed to go back.

My back is playing up. He made a low groaning sound. *Ah, ah ah.* I packed up our bags and stood up, my T-shirt still on, the cool wind making the fine hairs on my forearms spike up. I had known we would not stay long. I was quite amazed we were even there. I turned ready to walk back, wanting to show him how this was OK, not a problem, not a desperate last moment, not wanting to make him feel worse. Then he called my name. Faint, somewhat lost in the wind on the sand.

Come.

He had levered himself up and was standing looking down the coast, as it disappeared south towards Marco Island. The landmass was colourless, hazy now, the further south you looked, and the sand largely empty of its usual walkers as the wind began to whip our shins. Often, as now, with the Christmas holidays over, these were people a little older than us, couples, collecting shells, strolling, no children. And not always in couples, but alone, dragging an oxygen tank or accompanied by a nurse or carer. A big raincloud gathered out over the sea, hovering, tentatively. Andrew seized my hand. Motioned he wanted us to walk. Our familiar daily routine until the last month. His great pleasure, as he told me the first time he brought me to this place he loved. He had said we would hold hands up and down this beach and still be walking, limping there, when one of us had a colostomy bag and the other could no longer see. To his (and my) English snobbish sensibilities, the preposterous mansions and blocks built at ten-metre intervals down the beach were far too large, comical in their grandiosity. We had often amused ourselves, defining their architectural styles, Collier County Middle Renaissance, or Pelican Beach Baroque with a Nod to Doric Columns. *Perhaps you could build a Florentine Tudorbethan mansion,* I once said. He was a property developer, after all. Today there was no smiling, no laughter, nothing. After twenty or so steps, holding my hand tightly, he stopped.

All this, you know, all of this. All the bloody work I did. All the deals, all the money. It is so, so utterly, utterly unimportant. Meaningless. He gestured helplessly, not letting go of my hand.

I can't have any of it, it doesn't matter what I've done, how hard I've worked, what I've earned, none of it matters any more, none of it. Do you understand that I would be naked, with nothing, with nothing, if I could get rid of this fucking awful thing, darling, that is taking me? Can you understand it, Juliet, can you?

I could not reply, as my throat constricted with the crying that my body had to push back down somewhere. I held his hand and gently put my arm around his hips, feeling his pelvic bone jutting where the week before it had not.

He had gone straight to bed when we returned from our aborted visit to the ocean. The back pain that evening was excruciating and I hovered around him, going up and downstairs with my laptop to Google whether we could increase any of the doses of the drugs. Eventually I sat down on the duvet and stroked his head, as he lay, with his eyes closed. I asked him how bad it was, and he told me he could not describe it. I felt stricken, and guilty.

All I have is the boys' births really. I want to know how you feel, and I can't. He smiled and put his hand over mine.

I'm glad you can't imagine it. I don't know what giving birth feels like... But this feels like... nothing I can put into words. I love you so much that I would never ever want you to feel this.

He smiled sadly, but his eyes remained closed.

And from then we did not speak about the pain, as I felt too inadequate, with nothing to measure against. Our own levels of life, changing for ever.

21

The Last Time

By the evening of 27th of January, I am deeply, deeply worried, from the moment I am awake until I sleep. I have spent the day alone, downstairs, reading, making stupid blends in the juicer that he will not touch, calling the few people I am allowed to call and fantasising I am in a prison that I am going to be released from shortly. I want to be with my sons, with my mum, my dad, not here. I want Rachel. I want Jan. I am terrified. I can say absolutely nothing of this to anyone, because he is my responsibility. He has told members of his family who have tried to come and see him here that he does not want them. He wants everyone to stop making a fuss and leave him alone. I am all he wants, he says, all he needs. It feels an unbearably cruel decision to me. His determination is to believe that it isn't serious enough to panic his beloved children and family. I want to tell him how frightened I feel but I can't.

When someone cannot confront the possibility of their own death, an invidious situation presents itself.

Had I challenged Andrew's conscious denial of the gravity of the illness it would have been a betrayal of what he required from me. I was inveigled into a lie alongside him, which I think made his death all the more impossible to digest.

Repression is a most useful tool, repeats my analyst. Who I do tell that I am terrified. He says nothing, but I hear his regular breathing. Is he even listening?

What scares me is what is gone between Andrew and me, the ability to describe our feelings honestly and shamelessly to each other.

In the ensuing days, his pain reaches monstrous proportions, and my calls to Jan in London become more frequent, as do my calls, without telling Andrew, to the team at Smilow. They sound calm and tell me that when we return on the 2nd all of this will be reviewed.

The wait to return to Yale is bad. Hard. Andrew sleeps most of the day and little of the night. On 1st February, I pack as he directs me, preparing for the longed-for treatment. Andrew is shattered, making no attempt by now to disguise how wretched he feels. He sits in bed, the tips of his fingers on his temples, his iPad on his lap, discarded because he cannot concentrate as the pain rages through his body.

On the day of our departure, he takes over three hours to dress and he refuses my help, when I suggest I could put his socks on. He comes down the stairs of the apartment for the last time, slowly, but immaculate as always. I see how terribly thin he is with clothes on. There is a photograph I have of Andrew, taken as we waited for a taxi to collect us to take us to Fort Myers for the flight up. His skin is taut on his skull, his glasses large and overly big suddenly on his cheekbones. He has not shaved and his skin is dark and contoured. He has a hand on his chin; maybe I said something as I took the photo about the stubble. This would be his last flight. I can't remember a thing, cannot recollect any of it. Only the photo tells me where I was.

We arrived in the late afternoon to spend our last night together, in a hotel in Yale, called the Library, a pleasant enough place for visiting academics and parents of graduates. It occurred to me that we did not know how long we would be staying, but when I asked, the hotel could only guarantee two nights. Everything felt strange and impermanent suddenly.

This was to be his final night out of hospital, without oxygen being piped into his nose, and fluid dripped into his veins. We were due at Smilow at 8.30am the next morning. We cannot really at this point have still thought he would be given the immuno-therapy, but we persisted in pretending we did.

That night, a fresh snow carpeted itself over the towers and college roofs of Yale. I was starving and ordered us room service of chicken soup and dumplings almost as soon as we arrived, without asking him what he wanted, as I knew what the answer would be. He had lain down immediately on the bed in the other part of the suite, exhausted from the journey. The soup was delivered quickly, hot and smoking, to our room by a friendly young man who asked me how I was and how our journey had been and politely ignored the fact that one of us was invisible, yet the food was for two. Within minutes I heard the deep breathing of Andrew's sleep, and when I looked he was on his side, his hands prayer-like under his face, still fully clothed from the journey, only his glasses as usual neatly next to him. He had not even taken off his parka.

I remember the taste of the soup very distinctly. Over-distinctly. The mind has a way of processing sensory experiences when psychological content becomes overwhelming. I remember the whirling snow outside, its soundlessness, and the smell of the food, the lemongrass and ginger, the coriander leaves floating among pale matzo meal dumplings. Soft, tender chunks of chicken at the bottom of a fragrant broth. It was utterly delicious. I stoked myself, over-filling my stomach. I couldn't get enough, and when I had eaten mine, I started on Andrew's bowl, ripping up the black pumpernickel bread that accompanied both bowls and dipping it into the soup. The reverse mechanism of the anorectic, a defiant attempt not to feel unbearable feelings by savouring and tasting what I was putting into me.

Eventually, unable to read, and having covered Andrew with the duvet and turned out the light in the bedroom, I sat at a desk by the window and looked out on the nineteenth-century spires of Yale, not unlike my own university in England in the darkness, and wondered how this had happened as the snow came down harder and faster. My journey of adulthood ending in the one person I had found to love being so terribly sick, his life ebbing away. I heard him wake up, turning, aching, his sounds now undisguised agony. A deep, awful pain in his bones which I really did know then was the metastatic pain of the cancer burrowing deep in the marrow of his spine, his pelvis, his kidney, his liver, his brain.

Yet I could not comfort him, could not lie next to him now and tell him it would be all right. Anything I did now would not make any difference at all.

Early the next morning, 2nd February, I order an Uber to drive the short distance to Smilow. As usual we are there half an hour before the appointment. Andrew has been on time for everything in his life, and prefers to be a little early. *Jews always like to be early, darling; they worry the food will run out,* he sometimes says laughing at his own joke, but the joke is like a distant conversation from the past. We allow over an hour for a ten-minute journey. The snow is dangerously thick on the uncleared roads as the driver inches us the half-mile to Andrew's final destination. I see from the forensic iPhone records that I took a number of photos of him during these last days. His last time in a lift, his last moments in a taxi, on an escalator. All recorded. Did I know? Almost immediately, as we step into the atrium and take the lift up to the four-floor reception where the trial is based, it is clear that the immunotherapy will not be proceeding. They immediately notice the parlous state he is in. The nurses tell us within minutes he will be staying overnight for checks and rehydration, and within half an hour he is in a gown, on a drip and given oxygen.

I feel sick and panicked. I go back to the hotel to get what he would need in the hospital. His attempts to prevent his adult children arriving have failed and they text to say they have got on flights from London and will be with him shortly.

The fantasy that this was not an extremely serious situation is finally over.

The six days that followed were long and I find it hard to recall them day by day now as their slowness merged events, as the complexity of Andrew's condition grew. Andrew was increasingly exhausted, sedated, his mood strange and low, with moments when he would pull me to him, kissing me and telling me he was only quiet to conserve his energy, and that he loved me. *I have to be quiet to get myself out of here. All my energy must be to do that.* He underwent many procedures and saw numerous doctors, who gathered around his bed in semi-circles, all with lovely bedside manners, all charmed by Andrew still. One afternoon the hospital chaplain came, Episcopalian, kindly, large and wearing quirky purple Crocs with a violet polo clerical shirt. She introduced herself and sat down, laughing at Andrew's joke that things must be bad if she had been sent in, not least because he was Jewish. She suggested Andrew should tell me and his adult sons who had now arrived from London what he wanted and felt. *Imagine a situation where you might not get this chance, I know you feel you will but imagine you can't. We have this opportunity for you to speak to your family, to the people you love, to your sons and to Juliet. Tell them what you might want them to know.* He listened to her quietly. I still remember her kindness and warmth. Andrew asked her to come back and see him.

I have the notebook where I have written 11.15pm, 6th February 2015. I was beside his bed in a slippery vinyl chair I had already sat in for more or less three days.

Andrew was lying there, still and silent, his breathing steady, his eyes gently closed. His forehead was smooth, ironed out by the morphine. His full lips, always so enviably plump and rounded, and especially so in sleep, were calmly parted, and I felt my stomach suddenly liquefy with anxiety. His life and our life as a couple was ending. This was the moment that I started to record events, since it was the only way of making real what I could not believe.

For those of us with something to say but who are not writers, Borges remarks deftly, *What else is a blind man to do but to write?*

His death was sudden and unanticipated, early on Sunday 8th February. Today I cannot reconcile Andrew's death with his life. The chaos that ensued, the squalor, the indignity, the loss of control, the lack of planning. This was not Andrew. Forensic, quiet, methodical, calculating, charming, collected, unhurried. Cool. He was self-contained and in control, always. *Where there is doubt, let there be none.* His sweet mottos. *Don't worry, everything will be fine.* Now I often think, *Why did we not talk about his death?* I still only have hypotheses. One is that he was embarrassed about what it would feel like to die. The ultimate revealing, intimate physical act.

The impossible thought of dying when you don't want to, when you are not ready, and as it will transpire, when you least expect it, unprepared, in front of your wife, and others you will never meet, incomparable humiliation.

He died at 5.35am. I knew straight away, as his body started to writhe and his right leg flipped over his left, that he could no longer see me, though his eyes were open. A lot of people came rushing in with a machine. I called his children, who arrived within minutes from the nearby hotel they had booked into.

No one told me what to do, so for the first few minutes I hovered as a swarm of people crowded into his room. Then, when the scene became more violent, more desperate and urgent, I went outside to join his speechless children in the corridor.

Then a wait for him to die. It was around twenty minutes. I went between his room and the corridor, unable to stay in either. An unedifying, gruesome, ghastly scene. His death was not a going quietly, there were no eye-locked goodbyes, no hand holding, no stroking skin, no kisses, no drifting into a long sleep. I did not tell anyone but my mother what I saw for several months. I felt both guilty and angry that I was left in sole charge of this knowledge. We stood for the minutes while he was worked on, and this, the end of his life, will not leave me. I wish it could be unseen. All this would have to be thought through carefully in the months to come. My response to it and how I dealt with it I have tried to process, and yet still it makes little sense. I can spot trauma in my patients but it was harder to see in myself.

Immediately after he died, at his bed, I found myself casting around for what had just happened while five tired strangers in scrubs looked away and another expertly wheeled off the unused oxygen tank like a weary caddy. As he negotiated the narrow turning out of the room, another nurse high-fived him; presumably he was coming off his shift. *Hey Jason, how's it going, dude?* said someone at the head of the bed, to someone else, while Kacey, the nurse who had first come in when I had called out for help, looked at me and smiled.

Ma'am, you wanna leave the room so we can clean him up here, please. A cool order. Just like that. *Let's get him cleaned up here, please, guys,* she instructed her junior colleagues.

Then I remembered Kacey calling Andrew *buddy* in the last few hours, and in his final minutes too. *Buddy?* He had a name, he had a bloody name. *Hey buddy, buddy, come back here,* she screeched at him as I called her in when he started to die. Had she called him *Andrew,* this man she had been nursing for 24 hours solid, whose wife and children she had met, how could she possibly have coped, ushering in the violent ventilation equipment, which would be urgently, roughly pushed down his gagging throat, with no anaesthetic, in a desperate and hopeless attempt to keep him alive? She needed to keep her distance.

Something enormous and momentous had come into that room, minutes before, onto Andrew's bed, and taken him over as he struggled to breathe. In those last seconds, I felt what Freud termed 'the death instinct' as a presence in the room. *A death instinct, which is to lead organic life back into the inorganic state.* He had gone from being alive to being dead and this was the only way I could understand it. Death is impossible to comprehend. I felt it like an unimaginably immense, roaring bearing of some sort, coming to take him away, leaving him and everyone around him utterly impotent. Six hours before, he had been alive, warm, brown-eyed, handsome, breathing, looking at me. Now he was dead. How can a human being make sense of this?

I left the hospital 25 minutes later. This is how it ended.

Part III

22

The Beginning of Grief

I boarded my flight to London from JFK that night. Ironically, the flight Andrew and I had seats on. Other than that, nothing had gone to plan. The dose of the immunotherapy drugs had been due on 2nd February, and we planned to be back in London on the morning of the 9th, a week later. Our pair of seats had been reassigned to a couple about our age, who were toasting each other, arms crooked around wine glasses as I shuffled his and my bags into the overhead locker.

I sat down, once I had turned off his iPad, phone (difficult as I didn't have his passcode) and computer to comply with flying security. What did any of it matter, I remember thinking, and also, where *was* he? If you have ever lost a child at a check-out or in the playground of a park, you will know the feeling. Not heart stopping, but heart starting, heart pulsating, and an overwhelming feeling that something terrible is about to happen, in the two, three, four minutes before you find them again. I felt like that for the next seven hours, and would often do so again in the months to come. Where was he?

As the plane climbed through snow-strewn air, the black night gathered in and we flew up the coast, rocking from side to side with a strong tail-wind. Ten minutes or so into the flight, the map in front of my seat showed New Haven below me, and all I could think of was his body thousands of feet below me, no pulse and cold by now, I assumed, and not knowing where I was. He was dead but he might be worrying. Might he? I did not, *did not*, want him to be alone and scared without me. In a drawer somewhere. Andrew. *Andrew*. The incomprehensible nature of this. Added to which, the jeans I still wore that he had patted yesterday, my sleeve and wrist that he had stroked with his perfect healthy thumb last night. I was unable to lean back into my seat the entire six and a half hours, or to shut my eyes. As if I wanted to be ready to get off because there had been some mistake. I did not visit the lavatory or have a sip of water. Nothing went in or out of me. The grief had not even made its entrance at this point, but I knew something was coming.

I have never felt so bewildered.

At Heathrow, my father, standing next to the Costa Coffee, grave in a dark coat. *Juliet, oh dear, oh dear God*. He stopped speaking and took my arm. What do you say? What else do you say?

Andrew's driver from work had accompanied my father to Terminal 5, embarrassed, taciturn but wanting to help. He drove us back in Andrew's car, to Andrew's home – our home, a place that we shared and yet to which he would not return. I can't recall what we talked about. As I walked in through the familiar front door, it felt neither ours, nor mine. My mother was waiting there, with my sons, quiet and not at school. They looked at me hard and put their arms around my waist, holding onto me. *It's very sad, isn't it?* I remember saying, *It really is sad, isn't it, boys? Andrew loved you both so much, you know that, don't you?* They nodded, my nine-year-old looking at me, to see how I was, the seven-year-old just holding on, and looking anxiously at the giant box of Lego that had arrived in the kitchen, a present from my brother. The boys left the kitchen carrying the Lego out silently like a coffin. Their need to build did not escape me – would they be able to build a house now ours had been knocked down? Could they construct a new house for our new reduced family? My younger son said to me later that day when I went into their playroom, *The thing is, when adults are sad it's very hard, because you might just have to cry or sit there, but what I do is I play, and when I play I forget.*

That afternoon, up in our bedroom, I found my photocopied copy of 'Mourning and Melancholia', in Andrew's bedside table. I would not read it for quite a while; immersed as I was in the trauma of his death, and later the grief, I would have been unable to understand what Freud was saying. Grief, like depression, is only understandable once you are out of it. But a few months later I would pick it up again.

Four days after Andrew's death, a journalist friend of ours arrived at his Shiva, the Jewish 'wake', where anyone

who knew the deceased is invited to the house. Prayers
are said by a visiting rabbi and then immediate family
members can say something, after which people stay or
disperse into the night. I found it bizarre that within
minutes of the formalities being over, our drawing room
became a noisy meeting place, laughter echoing around
the room, hellos being said, warm greetings communi-
cated between people, many of whom I had never met.
The friend looked at me, amid the cacophonous sound,
then around the sitting room where she had recently sat
drinking wine with Andrew and me. I was still immo-
bile on my low mourner's stool, with my collar ripped
by a rabbi I did not know. She slowly shook her head
and raised her eyebrows, with a kind smile of disbelief on my behalf. (She had been unaware, like everyone
else, that he was ill.) *Write it all down,* she whispered,
looking around at the two hundred people still crowded
into our sitting room, more flooding down the stairs, a
box of kippahs from other people's bat and bar mitz-
vahs next to unsteady piles of prayer books by our front
door, from a synagogue I did not belong to, and that my
husband had not been to for years. The house filled each
night just before seven for four nights. I had been to
other Shivas, but never expected to host one in my own
home. I had never expected to be saying Kaddish (the
mourning prayer recited at every Shiva gathering, and
every Shabbat or Friday night service) in my own sitting
room. I followed her advice but I had already started
writing it down. There was nothing else to do.

It is five years now since he died and the battered

copy of 'Mourning and Melancholia' has always been next to me. With reading secondary texts, I have begun to understand it further. I understand the unfathomable distance between grief and mourning. I know that the capacity to put into words what has happened is progress, a sign that what has happened is becoming part of the story of my life, rather than the overwhelming event. Loss is the work of the therapist. It is everywhere, in almost every session with every patient. But loss and death are distinct experiences to be processed. Death is different from divorce, losing your job, selling a house you don't want to. These are losses, to be sure, which can provoke many states of mind.

But when the person you love most dies – the experience is unique.

In 1923, six years after the publication of 'Mourning and Melancholia', Freud published 'The Ego and the Id', which explored a concept that had been preoccupying him. His daughter Sophie had died tragically at the age of 28 three years previously. She was a victim of the Spanish flu, the great epidemic that swept the world from January 1918 in the aftermath of the First World War. Soon after, her little son, Heinele, Freud's grandson, would also die, aged four, from tuberculosis.

I find the loss very hard to bear. I don't think I have experienced such grief... I work out of sheer necessity; fundamentally everything has lost its meaning to me. (Letter 203.)

In 'The Ego and The Id' Freud acknowledged for the

first time that the pain of the loss of someone you love could never be fully overcome. It is an important concession, where he recognised something self-serving in his earlier idea that the ego might simply reinvest itself elsewhere and the relationship with the dead person end there. Too neat. You fall in love again and you forget the one you loved.

Freud had been severely and multiply bereaved and was able to see that the pain of bereavement would never entirely dissipate. In 1929, he wrote to his friend and colleague, the psychiatrist Ludwig Binswanger, after Binswanger's fourteen-year-old son died suddenly of meningitis.

11 April 1929

Vienna IX, Berggasse 19, 168F
Prof. Dr. Freud

Dear Dr. Binswanger,
I do not remember whether it was in 1912 or 1913 that I came to see you and found you so full of courage that you won forever a high place in my esteem. The years since then have, as you know, left me a fairly decrepit old man. I am no longer able to make the trip to come and take your hand.

My daughter who died would have been thirty-six today... We know that the acute sorrow we feel after such a loss will run its course, but also that we will remain inconsolable, and will never find

a substitute. No matter what may come to take
its place, even should it fill that place completely,
it yet remains something else. And that is how it
should be. It is the only way of perpetuating a love
that we do not want to abandon.

I would ask you please to remember me kindly
to your wife.

In unchanging friendship,
Your old Freud

Freud acknowledged what the bereaved fear but must accept – that we will never get over a dreadful loss. That the non-stop crying ceases, that you can talk to someone on a train or at a party about the fact that your husband is dead, and this happened when you were in your forties. That life is very much not what you expected at this stage. You can do all of this without breaking down in front of someone you don't know. The void is still there, however.

I did wonder, pretty desperately at times in the first two years, whether there was anything else I could do to help myself. I would very much have liked to have swallowed a pill to take the feeling away. Something to subdue my roaring, beating heart.

23

A Patient

Back in that frozen early spring of 2015, in the weeks after his death, when I closed my eyes to try and conjure him up, I didn't see all of him, just bits. This, it seems, is common, because to take him all in would have been too much. Sometimes it would be the back of his head, the camber of his shaven skull, or his hands, large-palmed, his fingers blunt and stocky, compared to mine. (We held hands a lot in life, our own mature crocodile of two, always searching for a palm to clutch.) Just as I fell into a feeling of profound relief and happiness at this memory, so I would find myself almost as fast coming to, with the equally profound despair that he was not back, that nothing had changed, that he was gone.

I learnt, once I was deeply into the tunnel of grief that runs alongside normal life that indulging in these thoughts made things worse; so I stopped.

There is another problem: grief fatigue. As the writer Rachel Cooke observes: *An additional danger lies in the fact – those who have experienced loss will know what I'm talking about – that no one wants to spend too much time with the bereaved, unless they're going through the same thing themselves. Here is fear and claustrophobia; here is an unremitting misery that can feel contagious.*

I tried, unsuccessfully with some people, who felt their own losses to be more considerable than mine, perhaps, not to give off what I felt. I am sure I was difficult. Who wants to be near the relentless havoc and misery of bereavement? A couple of people I considered close disappeared. A good friend was especially cruel, dropping me from her invitations, blocking me on her Instagram feed months after he died. I was childishly distraught. What was wrong with me? The truth is, for a long time, a relentless weight of injustice, anger and boredom was cut with a feeling that I could think of little except Andrew. So was it just me, or was it also the infectious nature of being near death for the living that pushed a few people away?

My older son as a small boy returning from a holiday once asked me whether now we had left Italy, would it still exist if he wasn't there? I sometimes find myself idly wondering this too – is New York really that frenetic, frantic, busy place if I cannot see it? I looked, spoke, did the same things as before Andrew was dead, but I was in a completely different world where I moved around in shadows. I was aware that I was not alone down there but I knew no one. There were as many of us as there had been in Andrew's Room Next Door, with new entrants joining daily, but every one of us alone in a bleak and unchanging underworld. No supporter group, online or offline, would have made any difference (though I admired the spirit of those that I found out about in my ad hoc nocturnal Googles). I was totally bound up in my grim solitude. It was unbearable to be with myself at times, but mostly it just felt like somewhere I wanted to get out of. An analogy is London's Underground system. Here you are aware of the Tube when you hear a train rattling below you, or perhaps when you pass a station. Much of the time, though, you forget about its existence until you are down there, tasting the different subterranean vinegary oxygen, feeling the whooshes of air around corners of tunnels, adopting the herd mentality of running for trains down tiled staircases. The smell is particular, familiar, not unbearable, but all the same, stagnant, breathed in and out by thousands of nostrils. And I am always so glad to leave a Tube station and get into the air.

After the first four months were over, I felt a relief at the prospect of summer. Naively, I thought that after that first awful spring the advent of May, June, then July might bring some slight relief, yet they did not. Instead fresh memories returned of the last summer, with him, when we had believed he was cured and we set off on what would be our last holiday. And a new thought had begun to percolate. That he was dead but could persecute me. In retrospect, I wonder whether I hated him at this point, but that this was such an unbearable feeling that I projected it onto him. Why was I allowed to be alive when he was not? How much more unfair could it be? We who had believed ourselves very different but entirely equal.

I endlessly recalled a conversation between us, towards the beginning of our relationship, long before his illness came along. It was mid-autumn, 2012, the sky darkening by six or so, the green of summer almost completely gone. We had been for a walk in Highgate Cemetery and passed the elaborate grave commissioned by a Jewish acquaintance of his, whose C of E wife was buried there. Later, Andrew said he had something he wanted to discuss with me. Where were we then? In a pub we liked near the heath, smoky panelling, glasses of wine in our hands, an early supper ordered. He, as usual when it was available, ordered sausage and mash, and rolled his eyes when I smiled. This was the moment, seemingly out of the blue, when he said we would need to organise where we were both to be buried, for I could not be buried next to him, and was I aware of this?

Andrew came from a United – or Orthodox – Jewish background, and I did not. He then said to me that in spite of this, we must be buried alongside each other. However, he had done some research and believed Highgate would be fine, because while there was only space there for immediate use, you could buy a plot in advance if you were over 80 or terminally ill. It was all rather hypothetical he said, given he was 49 and in amazingly good shape. *Yes,* I agreed, feeling perplexed by his urgency, pulling his large thumb and index finger into and around my palm playing with his nails, stroking my socked foot on his shoe on the uneven old floorboards. I stared absently at the fire in the grate, and looked around for our order. *Why are you even thinking about this now, though?* I remember saying. He said it was just important and we must make plans.

Yes, of course, of course. Whatever you want. I kissed him. *Of course.* Our waitress arrived with the food and put it in front of us. I immediately picked up my fork but his hand was on mine, stopping me.

I must be buried with you. If I die.

For around eighteen months after his death, I forbade myself these memories. I would not think about him unless he came unbidden into my mind, which was still very often. I tried to stop myself doing so, until it became spontaneous. A repression, but also, not allowing an addictive behaviour to wrench control from me. Not allowing a dead man to take hold of me – to take me away too. The only way I can describe this is that he was still dead in my mind at this point. That the over-whelming memory of him was his death, not his life.

I now believe those episodes of oblivion, when I couldn't remember how to drive, or found myself on the floor, or got into our wardrobe (and there were other incidents perhaps too shameful to remember), were grief at its absolute purest, its highest resolution, its most potent distillation. Grief is absence, despair, emptiness, abandonment each to an extreme degree, different from loneliness or solitude. It feels black; this is the similarity with depression Freud alludes to.

Three long years or so after his death, he would begin to come back to me, but in a different way – as an alive but dead man. He began to *be* again, which I now see as the mourning beginning.

Mourning is memory, recollection, sadness, but crucially the knowledge that the person was, at one point, there, loving, loved. They become reinternalised, come alive again in some way. The two came, for me, in sequence, although not discernable as stages. I was unable to begin to mourn Andrew until the grief had had its way with me. Grief was like living with a continuous voiding of my mind, like a sudden amnesia, what skiers call a wipe-out – of everything but the fact that I would never see him again. Grief, I now see, changes only with agonising, maddening stealth. When it chooses to release you, you are let up for a little light and air, out of the terrorist's lair, to see that others are moving on while you remain lassoed tight to your lost person, struggling not to be taken down with them, but unsure where else there is to go, and with no sense that anything will ever change. As a patient once said to me about their own long and dogged depression – when it had finally lifted, *When I am depressed I cannot imagine what not being depressed feels like, and when I am not depressed I cannot imagine depression.*

Grief was an obliterative darkness of endless fantasies that he could be dreamt back if I remembered him precisely enough, like an infantile wish fulfilment. Like a crying baby, *if I want my mother enough she will be here, she will make it better.* A crying baby whose mother does not come eventually stops crying. In life, he was what I thought I lived for, but dead, I did not want him to take me with him. My enormous anger and frustration delayed the mourning. My own neuroses, there decades before Andrew came along.

24

Grief and Mourning

Often in my consulting room, patients are surprised that nothing new is remembered. There is often an expectation that something may be dredged up and rendered clear or made relevant to explain their depression. But generally it doesn't happen in this way. It is more that the 'facts' are known unconsciously, and the feeling has got lost, just as 'Mourning and Melancholia' explains. Depressed patients often struggle to understand *what* is not there, as such a concept feels illogical, although there is a strong sense of a painful and frequently frightening absence.

With Andrew's death the events were straightforward: I knew what was lost – him – so the work has been to interpret the impact and effect of what happened. He was unlucky enough at 48, or 49, without a drag on a cigarette, to grow a miniscule tumour in his lung, which then started to disperse efficiently and imperceptibly around his body, at a speed that medicine could not keep up with. Today, there is still no cure for the cancer he had, a fairly common but determinedly murderous lung cancer.

We were both, from the day of diagnosis, as unprepared for illness as I suspect most healthy people in their forties are. Nothing unusual about that. Other than a healthy diet, exercising, drinking moderately, not smoking, avoiding stress. We did all of that, more or less, to the best of our abilities. So unlike depression, I knew what was gone, but what surprised me was that as a clinician, having seen death close up with the terminally ill and intimately bereaved in my consulting room, I thought it might be easier, more tolerable. This was not the case. Grief lasted much longer than any bout of depression I had ever suffered as a younger woman. Years longer. Only very slowly did it begin to change.

The grief terrorist guarding my cell became slacker, a tiny bit more lenient, allowing me out into a small yard for an hour or so, where I could see a blueish sky. He tossed me a chocolate bar, a cigarette – reminding me of what pleasure felt like. Perhaps even though he hated me, he had started to see a few good things about me. Perhaps he felt a bit better about life himself. Perhaps his humanity, beaten out of him, too, was returning. I was polite and quiet, getting on with my menial tasks and monotonous imprisoned existence.

And one day, a thought, from nowhere, *at least I am alive.* I now recognise that this was the point when the appalling grief began to lift and the mourning of my lost object – Andrew – could start. I felt for a long time that I was in a state of disbelief, not that he was dead, but that this was happening to me, and that I felt so trapped and controlled by his absence, which is so characteristic as Freud suggests of depression, except that the depressive does not understand the source of the loss.

The central relationship for most adults is the couple. When one of the two dies, its status is diminished, a widow is not a wife, and a widower is less than a husband. The dead person is taken away as a partner, but also as son, father, brother and friend. A mother lost her only son with Andrew's death. Four children lost their father. His sudden middle-aged passion for me was defiant. We found each other at just the wrong or just the right-time in our lives and his death provoked turmoil. Of course.

I was a second wife. A late entrant to his life and family. Others had loved him for decades before me. I knew from the beginning of our relationship that I would have to find and acknowledge my rightful place, which would only settle with time and experience. My parents divorced early in my childhood and I had a stepmother and stepfather. I was more than aware of the slow and complex blending of families that new marriages demand. But with his death, inevitably I was involved with the feelings of all those who had been part of his life. Possession, guilt, ambivalence, abandonment. This was a bereaved and shocked family that I was only beginning to get to know. It was another bomb detonating. For who owns a life? And who owns a death? Of course I wanted sole right to him, everything that our marriage vows had meant. Our right to each other, for us to endure as a couple.

It wouldn't be for me to choose the form of the service, place of his burial or his headstone. It was agonising to cede these last aspects of my promise to love and look after him, but correct. Only much later would I know that we as a couple had survived his death.

My work convinces me that there is no order in the unconscious. This seems especially so when dealing with loss. We move without awareness between our internal and external worlds, seeing, not seeing, stopping, starting, encountering resistances and barriers to comprehension. The unconscious feels dominating, overwhelming, and here what I experienced was an unworldly feeling of disassociation.

Yet, life, actually, did go on, in my usual, moderately organised and ordinary way, from almost 48 hours after he died. I think it does for most people. From my diary, from 11th February, I see the childminder's notes on what the children had had for tea, and her list of things I needed to buy, next to my notes on what needed replacing and doing (Persil, Lenor, Colgate, bananas, Muller Corners, chicken, basmati rice, carrots, eggs, orthodontist, chase up GP re ENT consultant appt for G's adenoids, packed lunch St Albans (Latin) school trip, window cleaner, put petrol in car, speak to Mum re vaccinations, Regent's Park football subs for F and G).

The woman at the corner shop smiled at me exactly as she had always done when I bought my paper, in a Pavlovian catatonia, three days after he died. She asked me how he and I were and had we been away? I am sure my smile was identical, and that I nodded in my usual fashion. It wasn't the moment to tell her that Andrew was dead, and that neither she nor I would ever see him again. She might have known his name. He might have known her name. He was the kind of man who bothered to find out people's names. She knew us both to smile at every day. He had seen her smile and smiled his easy, white-toothed, courteous smile back. A death leaves so many unanswered questions – from the banal to the unbearable. *Do you remember the man who used to hold my hand and wave to you? Did he know your name and had he told you his when he came into buy Haribo for the children alongside his* Observer *and* Sunday Times? These are not questions that can ever now be asked.

I thought this one night last week as I walked past her again, perched on her stool in front of the cigarettes, batteries and Rizla papers, behind the *Grazia, Hello* and lottery tickets. I was on my way to meet a colleague for supper. She was still there, though, on her stool, looking away when I passed. She probably does remember a man's face that she hasn't seen now for almost five years, somewhere in her memory. I soothe myself still that she has a recollection of him even if I will never be given access to it. This is the strangeness of a death, both how invisible and visible it is; that morning, 72 hours after he choked to death 3000 miles away in Connecticut, I walked out of her shop with my paper, as normal. Yet nothing was the same.

Being a close bystander to the accident of death robs

the survivor of their mind in all sorts of unexpected and particular ways, professional and personal. Common is not being able to read, as I have already mentioned. I could not read the paper I bought from the lady in the corner shop or anything else much, for two months. A clinical paper would have been impossible, as I could not take in more than a sentence, and then that would be forgotten by the time I had got to the next line. I remember finding it almost comical that one day... I could not read! I tried *Middlemarch* (to see if I could lose myself) and *Vogue* (for the pictures) and retained nothing.

I also felt watched by this new dead him whom I did not know. I remember fearing he might jump out from behind a door, or be in the shower when I got into it. I turned on lights to check he wasn't hiding in dark rooms, and I wondered if he was watching me like a voyeur in our bathroom, or like an intruder outside my bedroom window when I was sleeping.

One night, I got into a panic that there was someone – him? – in bed with me. I was very alarmed and crept over to the edge of the mattress and then fled up the stairs to my older son's bedroom, and locked the door and got in bed with him. He woke before me, his hair a blond whorl in his dark bedroom. He scrunched his nose and gently prodded me as he stood next to the bed, waking me from my deep sleep. His puzzled face and slowly shaking head. *Mum, why are you here? Why can't I get out?* I felt ashamed and made up a lie about a wasp in my room. This stage, which I now see it as

– was terribly frightening, the most scary in a way, a fear of actually seeing a malevolent zombie Andrew. This would be an Andrew whom I had never met, not the man I loved and yearned for – alive again and yet dead. I think now this newly hatched grief had a hallucinatory quality – the shock so enormous that my brain diverted from its normal functioning and went into a quietly stunned overdrive, started *seeing things*... Fortunately, this stage did not last very long.

The experience was also profoundly confounding and confusing, because I spent so much time simultan-eously wishing him back. The dead Andrew phase ended as my brain settled a little, beginning to absorb the reality. The shirt sniffing took much longer to conclude. However, in those first early months, I would still allow myself, could not stop myself, from fantasising during the day or while trying to fall asleep that he was about to walk in and then... there he was, walking towards me, his voice, his face, his body, him, all back again, *Hey, love, sweetheart, my darling*, those arms, those dry elbows, the familiar comforting smell of his breath. The dark hairs on his taut, pale-olive skin, his sturdy torso and – I wanted to breathe it in, breathe him into me.

I am interested now that I did not see him at this stage as a whole person, but rather one in parts – as I mentioned in the previous chapter. All these recollections of him were partial, in the way babies up to six months or so see only parts of their mothers. It would take a long time to be able to see him as I used to. Psychoanalytic theory offers us a view of human beings as initially only able to understand this primitive possibility of 'an other' via bits of them, the breast being the most fundamental way in which the baby is aware of its mother. The baby sees her as an extension of itself, just as a mother of a newborn may see the baby as completely separate and yet cannot bear to be apart from it in those early weeks.

A central preoccupation of psychoanalysis is the idea that, as human beings, we attempt from birth to make enduring and loving contact with a few other people in our lives, which almost inevitably also means tolerating loss, pain and disappointment. The death of someone you love is the enforced conclusion of that most basic instinct to love, the apparent ending of a relationship built over years, decades sometimes, the disappearance of the person you trust and rely on most for your well-being. I knew this but I did not know how wildly uncontrollable the destruction of this urge would be. Or how punitive. These are other characteristics it shares with depression. I did not know how long my internal world would be utterly transformed by Andrew's sudden disappearance, and how long it would take to recover some sight of it.

I knew theoretically, but not through personal experience, how trauma blocks mourning, hinders progress, binds the sufferer to the scene, corrupts memory and diminishes cognitive freedom and ease. With hindsight, I now see how impossible my attempts were to go back and tell my story, impose a trajectory on the three years following his death, see progress, improvement, recognition, and so forth. The feeling of progress that you have goes when life is interrupted by the death of the person you love the most. Moving forward stops. Stasis sets in. Time merges disconcertingly, slowing to nothing. As with depression, the mornings are the worst time as by evening there is some minor feeling of having got through another day.

People often comment assertively to the recently bereaved that the person is 'still with you'. This frustrated and irritated me. He wasn't with me at all. I couldn't even see him, let alone hear his voice. An email, one of many that arrived with heartfelt but occasionally clumsy messages, said, *Your other half is up there, looking down at you and taking care of you.* My son G saw my eyes roll as I read this and came over to stand behind me and read the screen. It became a whispered joke between us, articulated with an upward-pointing finger and a wink followed by an American-style fist-pump to the heart. This belief, that I should feel he was still there, troubled me for a long time. He had abandoned me!

An objective of emotional maturity is that as we grow towards individuality, we should be able to tolerate all our feelings, positive and negative. We desire, we disagree, we fall out, we fight, we despise, we recover, and with luck something is understood and we can love again. A charismatic Irish analyst friend says to her husband after a squabble, *During the next ten minutes I hate you and you probably hate me. I'll love you again when I stop feeling angry.* Death is the most brutal test of this definition of human relationships, because this time, the person does not come back. Our most primitive and early fantasies are brutally awakened and proved true. We are on our own, just as we have always feared. Nothing can be repaired.

I decided to train to work with couples three years ago and began to learn theoretically something I already knew: how enduringly contented couples always have a parental element to them as well as a robust sexual attachment. The capacity for desire and erotic compatibility must of course be accompanied by something more quotidian in order to live easily together in a house, with children, with jobs, with the ordinary every day. The sexual urge must be able to adapt to a different drive of compassion, when one person is unwell, following an operation, for example. An ability to pause the desire and nurse someone back to health needs to exist alongside a wish to engage in intimate, close intercourse. Andrew had looked after me well when I had been ill in ordinary ways, with a cold virus, recovering from minor surgery and a sprained ankle. I had reciprocated when his sporting injuries necessitated rehabilitative work and an operation.

Serious illness, terminal illness, though we did not speak of it as such, is a very different matter. His death was a perverse unravelling of all of that between us. I watched him subside in the last weeks to someone foreign to me. He became a stranger. A quiet, cut-off baby, not communicating with anyone, silent and absorbed by his body which could do little other than keep him alive. In the last weeks he could take in fluids and nourishment via his veins and be helped to accomplish the other basic tasks of excretion and sleep, via lactulose and morphine. Yet he would not let me help him with anything, and retained his dignity, on opiates or not. He did allow the nurses to look after him, and in the last week I felt a graceless jealousy that they could help him, while I could not. We had both cherished our distance and proximity as a couple and I see now he was holding onto that, while I desperately tried to forget it existed. The last time he would require help with a basic bodily function, I eagerly offered myself to the nurse as he ordered me away, his voice thin and reedy. *Get out, love. Get out.* The nurse cast a sympathetic, tired smile my way as I made myself scarce, tears scorching my eyes.

In this instinctive and protective primitive return to his body, he needed to preserve his remaining energy. The corollary of this necessary narcissism was that he switched off his emotional needs too, not requiring comfort in the last few days. In psychotherapy, this is called containment. To want me in those final hours and days must have been too much, too painful. He wanted to protect our coupledom too, which in retrospect was a gift to me as well as a terrifying regression on his part. The feeling of our existence in this most private of realms is protected still in my mind thanks to him.

25

The Couch

Forty-eight hours after Andrew's death, I lay down on my analyst's couch, beginning again in person, Monday to Friday, rather than intermittently on the phone, as it had been through January, my eighth year of psychoanalysis.

I continued without a break, five sessions a week. If the analysis had been hard while Andrew's illness engulfed us, the next part was not an experience I would recommend, and I think now was a mistake, on my, and perhaps the analyst's, part. But this is not a question I can ever ask now or have answered.

In the brutal wreckage of his death, I did not need the analyst's interpretations, could not take them in. With Andrew dead, I began to feel like a helpless infant, with everything I knew and trusted gone. I could feed and look after myself physically, but in other ways I had lost everything that made me feel like an adult.

The grief soaked through me, rinsing me of any capacity to think or reflect, damming access to my unconscious. The feeling of hopelessness grew as I felt the analyst probed my unconscious, complaining of blocks everywhere he went. I felt I was being judged harshly for my inability to move forward. I was vulnerable and deeply wounded. I wanted comfort and numbing, not to have my face rubbed into my suffering. I wanted Andrew. I felt even more pathetic that I could not move on towards becoming the analyst I had believed I would be, as training looked more and more unlikely as the months passed by, and my mood did not lift. I was being strangled by a pull backwards towards Andrew, that sadly I did not manage to convey to the analyst.

Bereavement needs better understanding as do its deleterious effects on the unconscious. In the first two years after Andrew's death, the more I continued dutifully to lie down on the couch for 50 minutes, the more I felt I should not be there. This was no simple resistance. A patient demonstrates resistance if they disagree with or cannot digest the analyst's attempt to interpret what is going on unconsciously. The fear is that an unconscious or hidden thought will be brought into the open. We talk about a patient having a strong or weak resistance depending on how open or closed they are to allowing the analyst to make sense of what they bring. I didn't feel there was anything hiding other than the tormentor that was the grief at that stage, but I kept on getting stuck and feeling horribly disapproved of by the analyst, which inevitably would draw the analysis to an end. No one can think when they feel negatively judged.

Naturally, most patients in psychotherapy or psychoanalysis have plenty of good reasons for not wanting to go to their sessions, and if they do manage to drag themselves there, they may still not wish to 'hear' or take in what the analyst believes is going on. The patient who consistently arrives late or indeed early, who rings the bell urgently several times or sends emails to cancel, is saying something, and the therapist has to work out what that is. It can be fear, or anger, or annoyance, about what the unconscious is throwing out at us, and it is the job of the therapist to explain these emotions.

Psychoanalysis in the aftermath of Andrew's death was impossible, though, because I could not access my own internal world. I knew I was exiled from normality. In my external world, I lived in the strangeness of a house, his house, our house, where he was not, yet where everything that was his was still in place. The impossibility of that, I think now. His toothbrush and socks next to mine.

After his death, I frequently felt that by being in analysis I was making myself worse, tormenting myself daily and getting completely stuck. There were good moments still between the analyst and me, days when I left his consulting room wishing I could have slept all day on his couch, so safe did it feel. I told him I had started to write and he encouraged me to continue. The analyst was well known, and in the last few months of the treatment I bought his latest book and carefully read it. It was brilliant, incisive, imaginative and further reinforced my feelings of inadequacy. In the final weeks, perhaps in the absence of anything else, and with a resigned acceptance that he could not help me, I often brought discussion of the book to the session, perhaps wanting to flatter him, make amends, show him gratitude for what we had had.

Female patients who become pregnant during an analysis frequently pause or 'interrupt' the treatment with the analyst's support. The theory is that the mother's whole attention should be with the baby, the merging of this new life with hers. The baby should be allowed to take over the mother's mind for a while at least. In a ghoulish and terrifying echo of this, the grief provoked by death precludes thought, messes up time, takes up space and detains the sufferer, demanding their full attention. I wish I had had more courage to tell my analyst that I needed to stop, or maybe come once a week, and sit opposite him, not lie down. I could not bear to spend any more time with my overwhelmingly active unconscious than I already felt forced to by Andrew. Days after his death, I told my analyst that I thought he had always known Andrew was going to die, but had listened to me all year as I tried to pretend, to hope, that this was not the case.

All I had was the information you gave me, he said. It was then that I realised I had been complicit in denying the possibility that he would die. It had simply been unthinkable.

This was perhaps the most helpful exchange I would have with him until the analysis ground to a quiet stalemate in May 2017. Another couple that ended unexpectedly.

26

Persistent and Complex

The Diagnostic and Statistical Manual of Mental Disorders, commonly known as the *DSM*, is now in its fifth edition. It was first published in the US in 1952 and it has become the psychiatrist's handbook, the go-to for psychopathologies and psychiatric disorders, or in lay terms, serious mental illnesses.

Among psychotherapists and psychoanalysts, nevertheless, it is a controversial publication. Are labels or definitions helpful to the sufferer? Is a drug company trying to find a cure for a new condition to make a profit? For over a thousand years, medicine has needed and relied on grouping together commonly occurring symptoms, and Freud and his followers were not strangers to this. They were, after all, doctors themselves. Freud's *Standard Edition* is full of names and descriptions of mental conditions, many of which have their modern translations in the *DSM* definitions – manic depression is what we now call bipolar disorder for example. Bereavement, however, is not an affliction or a disease that can be defined, which is why we find it, like depression, so difficult to be around. The *DSM* describes someone who after more than a year is still suffering as they were at the time of bereavement as having a *persistent complex bereavement disorder.*

After a year, I was having lunch with a couple I knew and suddenly rediscovered laughter, finding tears in my eyes at Tony's description of a disastrous holiday with a former girlfriend. I laughed for minutes and was unable to stop. It was the most pleasurable and familiar feeling. When it passed, I explained to them that I had not laughed like this for at least twelve months or longer. Something had found its way through. The fact that at that point I was no longer in the depths of overwhelming loss seems to me quite obvious, and I would not have expected anything else. Bereavement, persistent, complex and certainly as disorderly as mine would not have been helped by a diagnosis. It is simply what happens. The *DSM*'s definition seems bizarre – that grief and mourning should follow some timescale, like chicken pox, or recovery from an operation.

The 8th February 2015 became, and to an extent, still is my new measurement, because each day that has passed has enabled me to distance myself from his loss. I have counted in weeks, months, hundreds of days, comparing our time together with our time apart.

In 'Mourning and Melancholia', Freud states *The testing of reality, having shown that the loved object no longer exists, requires forthwith that all the libido shall be withdrawn from its attachments to this object.*

Withdrawn from its attachments to this object.

There have been times for most mothers or fathers when a child must be prised away, going to nursery, to school or when a babysitter comes to take over, or even at night when the kisses are done and it's time to sleep. Little fingers digging into my neck, clawing at me, or at my legs, *Don't go, Mummy, I need you, Don't leave me.*

You must, though, because a job, their education, a waiting supper table and your own sleep calls you away. The conflict remains. I have prised my own children away from me many times and it is a horrible feeling. For many months, I felt I was being dragged into the ground by Andrew. A persistent fantasy was that I would go back to his grave and dig up his coffin. I thought a lot about how deep I would have to dig, what kind of tools I would need. He would not let me go, and I was no match for his strength and size.

People would often say to me, consolingly, *It's been such a short period of time, it's so recent. Of course you will feel like this.* This, like most things, made me angry. Did they not realise what I had already got through, climbed, swum, waded, hurdled to just be here, alive?

27

The Truth

In the summer of 2017, Andrew's professor from Yale makes contact with me. We are on first-name terms, and have been since Andrew introduced us. Saul is coming to England, with a colleague, to UCL to give a lecture. Might we meet up?

Following Andrew's death, I received many communications from Smilow, to begin with handwritten cards and notes from some of the team who treated him, then emails from people whom we had only briefly met, whose names I could not remember. They were gentle and kind communications. The director of the hospital sent me a Catholic charm, noting this was not my religion but that she did not think that mattered and she hoped it would bring me some relief to know God would remember us regardless. I was moved and surprised that they bothered to do this, not least because it confirmed to me the impact that Andrew had made in such a short space of time. They talked of his strength, his character, his career, his care for his children, and for mine, and always of his great love for me. Evidently, on the two visits without me to the hospital, he had done a lot of talking. I responded to most of them, wanting more, wanting to know everything I could about every conversation that had been had, and the Smilow staff kindly replied. Saul had been to see me once before, for tea in our old house, in the autumn of 2015, bringing me a little watercolour print of Yale Medical School and talking to me of his teaching post at UCL and the work he was doing. I liked him, and something about him that first visit and the contact during our occasional emails connected me deeply to Andrew. It had bothered me that Saul had handed over Andrew's case to another professor the weekend he died as he was going to deliver a paper at a conference in Florida. I remember his last visit on the Friday afternoon, telling us we would see him again on Monday, and wanting to beg him to stay. I had a nagging feeling that we would need him over the next 48 hours, that no one could look after Andrew other than him.

So we set a date for a night to meet in London in July. It has rained but a sunny evening means we can have a drink outside. I have invited my father, my stepmother and a friend to join us – all academics. I want my father to meet Saul and for him to meet my dad, another professor. Perhaps I want to know that the conversation will not flag. My father is warm, reliable, interested in other people and has spent much of his career in the States. I know they will get on. Drinks are chinked and the talk in my warm garden is of Ivy League schools where both men and my stepmother have taught. My father's laugh begins to boom around the garden as confidences are shared. Saul has brought his associate, a pleasant woman about my age, and they both seem relaxed and happy to be there during this working trip. The conversation moves from Trump to Brexit, to the rise of the Far Right all over Europe, to an explanation of the demise of the Labour Party, to Saul's daughter's bat mitzvah and then, eventually, of course, as I know it will, to Saul's academic work and to cancer. It becomes clear my father, a statistician, wants to know in granular detail about how Saul measures his longitudinal studies and data collection. He sits, wine glass clasped between his palms in front of him, forehead furrowed in concentration, as Saul explains the aim of his work, and specifically these new drugs that can have miraculous effects on tumours, especially in the lung cancers Saul is interested in.

I feel a light wave of something wrong, a bit sick, and get up and down a lot. I am at the stove more than I need to be, given the supper is salads and cheese, all on the table. Eventually, I sit down, my stepmother fills my glass, offers me the bread bowl and smiles at me. I sense that the professor wants to say something, an update. The table quietens as the six of us fill our plates and begin to eat. Then Saul begins to speak. It turns out that in the two years since Andrew died, they have now established that this type of tumour – one of 23 different strains –would not have responded to immunotherapy. This is presented as very positive progress.

My father listens intently. He cups his chin in his

hand and leans in further. *Wow. Fascinating. How absolutely brilliant!*

I feel immediately very sad, and that if I do not get up again immediately there will be a horrifying explosion of tears at my dining table, not that I show it. As my father's cool enthusiasm for numbers continues, I go to fill a jug with water and get ice from the freezer. With my back to the table, I hear him ask Saul for forensic detail about how they have worked out that the drug does not work for this type of lung tumour. Saul begins to explain, and all four heads around the table are held in different poses of concentration.

What is dawning on me in those minutes is that the rush to America, for the second opinion, was a fool's gold.

It was guesswork, hunches, hopes, inventions, narratives, hearsay. Rubbish. Nonsense.

What Andrew put at a 40 per cent success rate was actually 0 per cent.

I wipe my eyes with a tea towel. I suddenly remember – and how on earth could I have forgotten this for over a year – that following the one dose of the immunotherapy drug on 6th January, everything started to deteriorate. Far from improving or lengthening this life, from that point he started slipping away. The last resort provided by the recommended second opinion.

I am in a state of disbelief at my father's reaction. He loved Andrew! Yet he receives Saul's information as a remarkable advance in another professor's research work. I feel betrayed. There is nothing to celebrate here; why is my father not sobbing with me here in the kitchen?

Almost two years later, I can understand there is nothing wrong with his reaction but it shows me how little he can know, will ever (I hope) know, of what grief is like.

Saul and his colleague leave at around ten, gifting me two Yale baseball caps and T-shirts for my boys, saying they hope I will come to Yale soon to see them and maybe visit Smilow. These Americans are good people, hard workers, clever, dedicated and kind. I like them, and everyone we met at Yale, very much. But I will never go to Smilow Hospital again. The idea is almost comical.

A week or so later, I write to Saul, to thank him for the presents, but also because I want to finally ask him what I have not been able to, which is what his prognosis was. I don't put it quite as starkly as this and begin the email telling him that I have been continuing to write articles on the consequences of bereavement, which I enclose. I have also been offered a contract for a book. I receive an email in reply.

Dear Juliet... You asked me about how advanced Andrew's disease was when we first saw him at Yale. It was stage 4.

Stage 4 means the disease has spread from the lung and traditionally the prognosis is very poor, as we know only too well... Of course, immunotherapy has changed the landscape but only for about 10-15% of patients – this is what we are trying to improve.

He promises he will check the old records next week and get back to me on *what the initial diagnosis was.* He ends with, *I hope we meet again.*

I never follow up because it was enough to know. Saul does not get back to me.

Stage 4 lung cancer remains unsurvivable. No one yet has survived it. No one. We both knew this, but we travelled in hope.

The following summer, in August 2018, I go to visit my father and stepmother at their summer place in France. It is boiling hot and I notice that my father is wearing a tatty sun-bleached baseball cap, pale blue rather than navy now, but with the word Yale clearly embroidered on it. I watch him napping in it every day, under the vine on their terrace. My stepmother tells me he dreads losing it and has the other one in reserve.

28

An Analysis

When I decided to resume psychoanalysis in January 2018, I felt very ambivalent. Partly it was because (I told myself) if I wanted to take up my place to train at the Institute of Psychoanalysis, I would have to go back to a schedule of five sessions a week, so I had better get on with it.

But the new analyst's first and only comment was that I had not begun to mourn Andrew. I stared blankly at the ceiling of a new room and tried to take it in.

Andrew died three years ago, I insisted, he was wrong, I had done a lot of processing and was ready to move on. Hence coming back to psychoanalysis, even though it hadn't worked out with the former analyst. The new analyst was quiet for around 30 minutes and right at the end said only, *You have been traumatised. You have been stuck with your grief. You are back to see if I can really listen and understand what you are saying, and what you feel.*

Trauma means a profound shock. The shock can be to the body – a car crash, for example, or to the mind

– a sudden death of someone beloved. Sometimes both at the same time. Either way it is an injury that can leave both broken limbs and psychic breakage. Wounds occur daily to human beings. You have only to watch the spectrum of emotions a four-year-old goes through in a morning's play to see that. We learn to regulate, to moderate our responses to what upsets us, and to understand that we will get over things, digest them, process thoughts and ultimately forget. Most emotional wounds resolve, but some linger. When something unforeseen and incomprehensible happens, when the stimulus is strong enough – a death, for example – the mind may not be able to process the event.

Trauma feels like a mind of its own. As if the mind has a mind of its own. A mind that has nothing to do with the owner. For example, a repetition compulsion can begin with the victim relentlessly revisiting the scene of the trauma. (This was my experience of Andrew's death scene, a strange replaying again and again of those minutes on his hospital bed, unlike anything else I had ever experienced.)

I left the session and stomped angrily to my car. How could he diminish everything I had been through and got through? Then I realised it was true. *You were traumatised. You have been stuck in your grief.* These few words somehow unlocked me. I soon felt grateful for his apparently straightforward diagnosis. A new analysis began and with it the prospect of a new way of thinking about what the grief had done to me and also, I believed, the possibility of working out where I was in relation to

'Mourning and Melancholia'. And I began to feel very different, though I still missed Andrew chronically.

Yet from that day onwards it was often in the most fleeting moments of the day that I began to notice Andrew's absence – in a way that amazed and surprised me. I would feel a little pleasure, a shiver of something good and reassuring when I remembered him. I emptied the dishwasher and put the mug with G (my older son's initial) on the shelf and recalled buying all four – one for me, one for him, one each for the children. They are plain, white with one black letter on the front. The A sits boldly at the front of the cupboard when I push the J in next to it.

I looked for a pair of shoes in a hurry and finally pulled out the bottom rung of my shoe shelves where his initialled velvet slippers lay, neatly together, next to my lost pumps. The slippers are worn, the gold stitching frayed, the heel a little broken down. They were a present from a friend, tongue-in-cheek, regal red, the sort of thing a king might wear. He always wore them as his feet were often cold. *My Jewish prince,* I said, as they were the most comical items, especially worn with surgical stockings after his hernia surgery. I remember him throwing his head back and dancing a little jig. I smiled at the memory.

My sons and I moved house around seventeen months after his death. I was very ready to leave the mausoleum it felt our family home had become. As with any move there was work to do. A new consulting room for me, new bedrooms for us all, and above all, a new place to return to each night and wake up in each morning. I fervently hoped there wouldn't be so much of Andrew in the new place. One afternoon, as I was unpacking boxes and filling the new bookshelves, a note fell out of my old copy of *Middlemarch*. A torn piece of graph paper with a list of things he had to do one day, his slightly curly writing, a couple of spelling mistakes. He often asked how to spell words. I remember this suddenly. *Love, substantiate?* His face looking at me, listing to the side. *Tell me, clever clogs.*

Every day now the little wooden keyring I gave him gets trapped between my car key and the alarm fob of our new house, and each time I think I must get a new one but then I untangle it and see 'I remember you' that I had had carved into one side and 'I see you' that he had got carved into the other.

And I do now, both remember and see. I remember him making tea, the bag in together with the milk and a scant teaspoon of sugar if he thought I wasn't watching. Then how he would sit, at the kitchen table, iPad in hand, or wanting to talk to me, or watch me. Our mornings, he and I up before the children, me generally finding him awake next to me, needing only five to six hours sleep, the papers digested, or lying on the sofa in the sitting room on the first floor. I would collect him on the way down to the kitchen, pulling his hand down the stairs after me. That half-hour together, often discussing his work, his feelings about someone, mine, a plan, a holiday, supper. The sleepy boys coming down, sometimes me carrying my younger son from the top floor. Every Wednesday my mother coming to spend the day with us, his warm greeting to her, *Say hello to Granny, boys.* The orderly way he liked to live, the respect he felt for all our roles.

His notes, I thought, I had largely collected, but still they surprised me. Out they fell, here and there. The note-making was random, in different little note-books, and each new one pleases me, surprises me.

YOU YOU YOU YOU YOU YOU YOU.

I long to call you Mrs Rosenfeld. I long for you actually. Til tonight. A

Now they began to feel like posthumous declarations of his happiness, of our happiness, not messages from wherever he has ended up, which, in my secular mind, means nowhere, and everywhere.

After around 36 months, the grief began to subside and the mourning could begin. I read an account by a mother of a child killed at Dunblane who recounted that after about five years her life began to feel liveable. So maybe 36 months for a husband. Freud has not been specific, but if I add a year on to compensate for the century that has elapsed since he wrote the paper, and longer life expectancies, I thought to myself that perhaps I am on some sort of course. I felt different because mourning is a different state to grief. It does not dominate, takes up less space. I felt sad, but also, for the first time, able to remember him with pleasure. Able to remember aspects of how I loved him and more importantly how he loved me. Mourning signalled the overwhelming shock receding, and life beginning to feel ordinary again.

Sometimes I have thought if I had had the choice, never to have met him, never to have had our friendship, our love affair, our marriage, our great solid life together and thus not have known the desperation of losing him, what would I have chosen?

At times I have thought it would have been better. Had I never known him, I would not have stumbled into the excruciating nightmare of solitude, desperate, angry pain that he put me through. He is, after all, entirely responsible for the worst experience of my life. I paid for three and a half years of happiness with three and a half years of despair. But this, as the analyst commented, is not reality. That was never a choice open to me.

As time passed and I began to be able to refer myself more helpfully back to psychoanalytic theory, more changes came. My analysis has become once again, what it was, an analysis, and I am interested by it. It did involve a change of analyst, however. In a way this was a significant loss – the end of a love of sorts, although this could be replaced. The old analyst is not forgotten, nor our work together. After a few months, a slow shrugging-off of the heavy shawl of grief commences once I am certain the new analyst has understood how appalling the experience has been. I see I need not have worried.

This was a terrible agonising event for you and for him, a horrible tragedy. He sounds as if he loved you very much, and he sounds as if he was a very good, kind, loving man.

The new analyst's strong foreign accent is at times difficult to understand, but he is reassuring. I know, he knows, what Andrew meant to me in life. The new job of the analysis is now to bring me back to life.

One day, during a session, I am startled to recall the conversation, a few months after we met, at the pub about burial. I tell the analyst what Andrew actually said.

I just want to be buried with you. If I die. Which I won't.

I comment to the analyst how interesting it is that I forgot this last sentence. Perhaps even then, well, well before the cancer was diagnosed, this much I knew. I knew he could not be assured of this. None of us can.

This analyst did not know Andrew alive, but three years after his death helped me to discover him alive again. By this I mean that I mourn, not grieve, Andrew. As its participants know, psychoanalysis is frequently a procedure that delivers more disquieting knowledge, indeed as many new queries, as it supplies answers. A bereaved person may not be able to take in any more disquieting knowledge than they already have.

As Gregorio Kohon writes, *One cannot learn about psychoanalysis, one can only learn from psycho-analysis.* (1999)

29

Two Shirts, Summer 2018

I am heading onto the heath on a late-June morning. It is 6.35 and I have left the boys in bed, with a note on the kitchen table: *I will be back at 7.15 for breakfast, Mum.* I pass some determined swimmers already in the mixed pond and turn right towards Parliament Hill, my breath quickly becoming more laboured as I ascend the first gentle slope. I run through a heavily copsed avenue, where a dirty sleeping bag lies slug-like on a bench to my left. A vulnerable little tuft of hair pokes out. It has been a warm night and my mind is unselfconscious, free-associating. *Would it be so bad to have been out here last night? Was it a man or a woman? Who is the person in the bag? Do they have a wife? Children? What happened?* I am aware my head feels empty, not worried about anything, not feeling something dreadful is about to happen. This is still an unusual feeling for me. Nothing is particularly bothering me, thoughts are coming and going, there is space once again. I have allowed enough time to run, to shower, to get the boys up, fed and to school, and back for supervision on Skype at nine and for patients starting at 10.30. The day feels in order.

The Heath at this early stage of summer is a green whorl, louche in its excess with a haze hovering over a few chatting dog walkers and sweating runners who admire the view down over the city. I look too, marvelling as always as London spreads out below. The path is flat and shrouded on both sides by green, and I pass two fellow women joggers and we nod and grimace at each other.

I am still pulling my limbs out of sleep, and find myself wondering whether I am aging, my fitness declining, since a slight pain in my knees jars them as I cross down over the Heath, towards the first of the ponds. The thought is gone by the time I decide to turn left and make for Kenwood, breaking into more of a run now as I descend towards the Women's Pond. I turn and pant my way up the side of the woods separating Hampstead from Highgate until I am on the wide central avenue in front of Kenwood House, brilliant in its chalky whiteness. I carry on down the avenue of beeches, past huge tropical-coloured rhododendrums, past more dogs with their walkers. I take a sharp left, past the large Henry Moore sculpture, and race down, wanting to make a huge loop. Now I can see no one and I am in a walkway that feels more like a tunnel, an escarpment of yews, vine and hollybushes.

Then, quite suddenly, I remember walking with him there, in the same place.

It was high summer, a late-July evening in 2013 and

we had walked past Kenwood, then down to the lake and its strange folly and into the dark undergrowth that separates the Kenwood estate from the rest of the heath. I grasped for his hand in the darkness and felt it, warm and stroking my palm, pulling me behind him over the sandy limestone path, where anything might happen, anyone might jump out.

It's so dark, I said.

Definitely. He replied.

It's so dark Andrew. Anything could happen.

But it won't, because I am here, and so are you. He was wearing a pair of jeans and a white shirt, rolled up at the elbows, tucked into them. His dark-brown eyes were invisible in the blackness.

Really? I said.

Really. Love, we will be fine. We will be fine. I promise you.

He took my hand and pulled me with him along the lane, up out onto the large expanse of heathland between Highgate and Hampstead, limpid straw-grey yellow now in the moonlight, the city's skyline brilliant in front of us, the lights west across from the BT Tower, to the Hilton next to Hyde Park, miniscule, studded, glittering, red, green, blue and strobing yellow. We strode through wheaty grass until we reached Parliament Hill, then continued down to the lower reaches of Hampstead, where I would live, without him, five years later.

There is an idea in psychoanalysis that everything is there in the first session, if only it could be interpreted. Of course, it cannot.

With him, when I met him, I stopped being scared of many things, and without him I at first thought the old terrors would return. Except they didn't.

On a good day now, I think of him perhaps twenty, thirty times. It may sound a lot, but it is nothing compared to what it was. It was every minute of every hour I was awake for many months, more in the first six months, most of every minute. He was constantly in my head, dead, angry, beseeching. That part seems largely if not entirely over, and this is an enormous relief. But I still think about him – he still, daily, forces his way in. I realise that I want to be in charge of when I think about him, rather than the other way round. Maybe one day this will be how it is.

I continued to read 'Mourning and Melancholia', poring over it until I knew it almost by heart. It still had, and has, profound resonance for me, but as I started to feel different so I realised that I didn't agree with Freud entirely. The idea that I would only finally recover from the loss of my love affair with Andrew when I fell in love with someone else didn't feel believable. I would never not be in love with Andrew. *Yes, perhaps. But maybe one day you will have to find a way to make space for someone else too,* suggested the analyst. I didn't argue but lay silently taking in, for the first time, the possibility of this idea.

The summer of 2018 is strange and startling in its warmth. Observing the Heath from our house has been fun for the boys and me. *Like a beach with no sea,* says my son F. It is full of pale bodies every day, lying on their sand-less grassy mattress, and the three khaki-green swimming ponds full of swimmers. Now in August we are preparing to go away for two weeks ourselves, but I have been postponing several tasks that have to be done before we leave for a number of reasons, including the sheer boredom of name-taping every item my older son will need for his new school. Both boys have been away overnight at sleepovers, and I spend the day alone.

I am in our new house, somewhere where Andrew will never set foot. There has been a lot of work to do, and the decorators have finally finished after much discussion and what my sons call 'problematising'. It feels as if it has gone on so long, and indeed it has – so long – that the season has changed. The new radiators have yet to be tested, the door to the garden is left open and the roses I brought from our old garden and replanted when we moved in here are now blooming. I have, I estimate, seven hours to go up to the top floor and tackle the name-tapes and sort out the clothes. I talk to my mother, to a friend, write up some patient notes, read a bit of the paper, buy some lettuce and cherries at the fruit-and-veg stall by the station, have a coffee, come back, fiddle around in the garden and then, finally unable to distract myself any longer, go upstairs to gaze at the huge pile of clothes that the rebuilding of some outdated fitted wardrobes has left me with.

I have been ignoring this growing collection of carefully folded clothes, which the decorator has been dutifully putting onto the double bed in the spare room. I see the boys have been plucking garments from it as and when they have seen fit. I walk around it, sipping at my tea, wondering where to start.

I know I cannot put it off any longer and I begin bustling up and down the flight of stairs in our narrow house, setting Radio 4 on both floors. I designate piles to separate places.

Up and down I go, bagging up clothes for a friend's small son who is going to my boys' school, navy and white clothes for a friend's toddler daughter who refuses to dress in pink and clothes of mine for my two cousins, and my mum and aunt who like my cast-offs. There is also a bag for Oxfam into which go the outgrown or now displeasing cartoon character clothing the boys briefly loved, inflammable and sweat inducing, for some other mother to dislike.

There is a small Tottenham Hotspur jacket that my son F has not worn for a long time. I look at it, and remember him, hair still that late-toddlerhood peroxide blond, ringlets to his shoulders, modelling it for Andrew, a Spurs fan. Then there are G's white vests, the exact size of his thin boy's ribcage, which is now filling out, as muscles and fat start to imperceptibly change him from a child to a teenager. Their outgrown pants are in neat triangular piles, one had to have Y fronts, the other slips. There are bundles of our skiing socks, thermal leggings, salopettes, and our helmets and goggles. There are two little linen suits, which they wore for our wedding, now Lilliputian small. There are also two tiny velvet-collared navy coats, which my father improbably went to buy at Harrods, the morning of Andrew's swiftly arranged burial. Size age 8 and 10, bought so they could grow into them. Of course, they never put them on again. Gradually I begin to make inroads.

After an hour I sit down. I feel flooded with memories and I am suddenly remembering our old house and the top floor with its views of the park where the children slept above us, a large white tiled bathroom with their rubber ducks, little towelling dressing gowns, Johnson's shampoo and nit combs. The separation of space worked for us all, somehow leaving us free to be a new couple below them.

I know what I am dreading seeing, and why I have been putting this clear out off for so long.

Underneath everything, as I knew they would be, are Andrew's clothes. I have not seen these for three years now. I take a breath in and begin to look. Here are his favourite jerseys. A fine maroon-coloured jersey of merino wool, and then a grey Joseph cardigan. A blue cashmere V-neck that we bought together. These are the clothes of a man now dead longer than he owned them. I stroke the maroon jumper, try it on, then pull it off. I fold them up and put them into the new wardrobe where I have left an empty drawer for his things. I continue to go through, sorting, knowing that a sweatshirt he loved will please G, even if it is a little big.

Then I see the white shirts. Unwashed still. I have all but forgotten my crazed love affair with these two cotton garments until this moment. I grab them both and smell them quickly everywhere, everywhere I used to, the wrists, under the arms, the collar, the chest.

There is nothing.

Were the shirts like a baby's 'transitional objects'? Donald Winnicott coined this term for a toy or piece of comforting material that a baby uses as it shifts from believing itself to be a part of its mother, to a person who can have relationships with other 'objects', the psychoanalytic term for people. The baby holds onto or sucks its dummy, or clutches a scrap of its mother's dress, to maintain the illusion of a connection with her, even when she is not present.

I, like a child growing up and ready for independence but also capable of knowing their mother still exists even when they goes off to big school, have also outgrown them.

I feel an intense draw towards him, impossible to describe as I shut the wardrobe and feel tears welling. As the feeling rises, I finally see his face fully, staring at me, looking into my eyes. In turn I look down at his entire body, his chest, in a dark linen shirt he wore on our last journey up to Yale, his skin olive-brown, his Levis belted and black loafers on his feet. I walk up to him and look into his dark eyes. He does not smile but continues to look at me, taking me in and allowing me to do the same. He does not speak and his lips do not part but are still, as are mine. I have no need for words, but I am able, finally, to take him in, his whole body, and I see him perfectly. We stand together, not touching.

Then he is gone, or the moment is over. Was this a waking or lucid dream? The first, an involuntary dream occurring while someone is conscious; the second, when someone is aware they are dreaming. Did it come from my conscious or unconscious mind? Was it a hallucination – a psychotic symptom when someone sees or hears something which isn't there? I don't know, but I was not at all frightened by what I saw. On the contrary. The thought of it still brings me something akin to bodily pleasure.

In *A Grief Observed*, written in the aftermath of his wife Helen's death, CS Lewis wrote, *And suddenly, at the very moment when, so far, I mourned H least, I remembered her best. Indeed it was something almost better than memory; an instantaneous unanswerable impression.*

This is the clearest explanation of what I experienced and I now see it as a sign that my mourning was abating.

Since Andrew died, I realise I have been prone to a number of new, strange experiences. Not one disturbed me, other than the fear of him coming back dead, which ceased relatively quickly. What disturbed me was the tremendous and permanent shock of his departure. This was what truly seemed mad. That a live human being could simply disappear. The experience in our spare room filled me with a sense of longing, but also reassurance. We will never meet again, this much I do know, but I also know he will never, ever leave me. Sometimes, though, usually between three and four in the morning, when nothing makes sense, I am prone to wondering whether we paid a devastatingly high price for what we were given.

Did we selfishly love each other too much? Were we too happy? Were his cancer and death a punishment for our excessive pleasure? In those bleak moments in the dark, I can still lose my reason and think there can be no pleasure without pain. I can also summon him back in the small hours before dawn. I can imagine his arms around me, the feel of every inch of him telling me to go back to sleep or laughing at a joke. I see him perfectly and I can look right into his eyes again, feel his hand holding mine. He can put me to sleep when my own meandering wakeful thoughts cannot. I have him back, and yet I don't.

So Freud was right; I cannot ever give up my love for him, which means the sadness he is no longer alive must also be retained. Freud, in 1923, wrote in a letter following his grandson Heinele's death that he would never get over the loss. *He meant the future to me and thus has taken the future away with him.*

The impact of Andrew's death has been profound, perhaps as profound as the impact of his life. Because of my job I expected to understand what his death would do to me but I did not. Because death this close *has* to be experienced to be understood. Perhaps this is why the analyst with his neutral stance could not comfort me. I had no sense at all that he knew how I really felt, how absolutely desperate I was after Andrew's sudden departure from my life. His death would mark the end of my capacity to be analysed for a period of time, another loss, but a necessary one.

In writing this book I am doing what I wished

someone might have done for me. To say, there is no remedy for this, no plan, no stages, no 'grief-work', no antidote. There is only you, and your loss. And time. And even that may take for ever, longer than you have left to live. The mourning, in my case, has not ended. It won't. But the act of writing, as various commentators have observed, may in itself be an important aspect of moving on. I did not realise this until a few months ago, as I began to finish this book. Writing confirmed that I was alive. It preserved him for me and now confers remembrance on him.

In *To the Lighthouse*, Virginia Woolf describes how Lily, her heroine, thinks about Mrs Ramsay, the mother figure who has died ten years previously. Lily begins *feeling the old horror come back – to want and want and not to have. And then, quietly, as if she refrained, that too become part of ordinary experience, was on the level with the chair, with the table.*

Perhaps Freud looked at himself, as he did his theories, as work in progress, and with the benefit of his experience concluded that when someone you have deeply loved dies they never really leave you, and you can never quite leave them, or ever quite shed the frustration and sadness that they are both there and no longer there. You can, however, move on, and continue your own life.

I turn back to the black bags, ready to be given to their new owners. I will take one white shirt with me, downstairs to the laundry, when I finish, leaving its twin upstairs.

I open my wardrobe filled with my winter clothes and I put the white shirt in there, between a jacket and the black winter coat I wore to his burial. I check the rest of the rail, see that everything is well spaced, clean, ready for work again at the beginning of September. There are sandalwood sachets hanging down at equal intervals, bought by him, in bulk. I smile. Maybe I have learnt something from the orderly man I briefly shared my life with. Now I see the shirts differently too. They are the transitional objects that helped me to manage the increasing distance between Andrew and me, just as the baby manages to bear the absence of its mother as it is weaned and put to bed alone. I too had to learn (again) to go to bed alone. One of the boys will wear the shirt one day I hope.

It is now early evening, and there is birdsong and sunlight coming in through the windows. The Heath opposite our house is still filled with people clutching bags of food and bottles of beer and wine for picnics under the luminous green trees. Others are leaving, with towels slung over their shoulders, heading for the Overground train station. I hear my sons screaming with laughter as they play on the Xbox downstairs, and their excitement suddenly sounds life-giving, joyful and intoxicating to me.

I make my way down to them. A friend will be here soon for supper and I need to get things ready.

A flower that blooms only for a single night does not seem to us on that account less lovely.

Freud, from 'On Transience', 1915.

Afterword

A mass bereavement

It is midday, a sharp spring Monday in April 2021, and I am in the car with my father heading on to the A1, directed by the sat nav. We have just left the hospital in Enfield where I've had my second vaccine along with other mental health workers. The jab means I can finally forgo Zoom, Skype and telephone sessions and see patients in my consulting room again. Some I have never met in person, and some are people who 15 months ago had husbands, wives, and partners.

The Office of National Statistics records that 24,257 people were widowed between December 2019 and April 2021. But this figure doesn't account for those in unmarried relationships, and the truth is we will never know how many men and women the virus bereaved.

Last week in a clinical group meeting I was told of a patient whose husband was ventilated for four months before his machine was switched off. The psychotherapist treating this woman said he was very concerned about her state of mind. So am I, still, and I can't stop thinking about her. (She was 45, he 52, a fit, slim man the notes said.)

My colleagues and I are all worried about how our patients are coping, and concerned by how many referrals we all receive, daily now. I am frustrated I cannot even offer a single assessment and spend hours most weeks contacting other psychotherapists to see if they have vacancies, which they don't. A despairing mood permeates supervision meetings and the low-fee clinic where I trained has a hopelessly long waiting list.

Worry is in the air generally about mental health provision, and how bad this time has been psychologically for the young, the elderly, the under-privileged, and the lonely. Politicians and the media talk of a tsunami of mental health problems as a result of the pandemic but I wonder if its effects will change anything. The NHS has managed the epidemiological catastrophe, but the psychological consequences are neither funded, nor yet known.

The number of cases, and deaths, have become the thermometer which gauges how quickly life will return to normal. To begin with, photos were flashed up nightly on the television screen, and I wondered what this moment of recognition might mean to someone, whether it felt strange or comforting, or neither. Grief doesn't respond to much. It is like an imperious consultant, delivering the worst news with no bedside manner, and moving without a goodbye onto the next bed. Again, and again and again.

But each story is someone's story. The story of two people who loved each other more than anyone else. The story of the devastating impact of one of them dying before the other, leaving the other behind. The story of a family decimated. How could we expect anything else? And yet, each time, it is devastating. Grief is not a mental health issue in the same way as depression or anxiety. But it is a profound psychological wound, one of the most bleakly transformative events a human being can experience. Its effects last for years, sometimes longer than a person has left to live.

Today my father and I still have another destination to get to, and he is solicitous, asking if I am ok to drive and whether my arm is hurting yet. He is accompanying me on the journey that I make, without fail, three times a year. So here we are, speeding along the complex artery of motorways that pulse around the edges of London. I reassure him I am fine, and he nods and looks out of the window, pointing now at a cathedral on the horizon that he says is St Albans. The light traffic allows us to accelerate past Barnet, Watford, Edgware, Elstree. The land is flat, gradually emptying and we are on a high plain. Pylons and indistinct two-storey housing estates are greying blotches as far as the eye can see, with the earliest green glow of summer daubed in patches between them.

After twenty minutes or so we have reached our destination and I have to turn sharply between two high, forbidding gates into a small carpark. A collection of Portakabins is in front of us. I turn off the engine and turn to him, but as I do so my eye is caught by an open door where four simple wooden coffins are neatly piled.

Ready?

I'll stay here love. You go. Go and see Andrew, go and say what you want to say alone.

For a moment I feel a childish pang of abandonment. I pause.

Really? Don't you want to come?

My father smiles and gently taps my hand.

No, go and see him alone. I'm fine. I've got plenty of things to do – take your time.

I zip up my jacket against the wind and walk past the '60s prayer hall with steel doors, ahead of the two huge burial grounds that border the sides of this small cluster of concrete, purpose-built buildings. An awning covers the walkway down to the border of roses that are still not out, and ahead of me are a couple of men arm-in-arm, holding on to their kippahs as they walk. I cannot remember much of the day of his burial, but I do remember the strangeness of many friends standing around this concreted square, looking at me, as I walked back to the car with Andrew's parents. Like a bizarre party, outdoors, freezing, where the host doesn't speak to anyone and doesn't smile. I remember thinking it was a dream, questioning whether it was happening. Perhaps I was calmly dissociative. I now know that I was traumatised. I had, after all, watched Andrew shriek his way to death.

Each time I come here, I am overwhelmed by the scale of the place – how many new headstones and open plots there seem to be. The sheer number means I cannot work out where I am for a minute or so. The graves stretch as far as the perimeter of the field and I tighten my scarf around my neck as the breeze is icy, despite the sunshine. I look for the number of the section he is buried in and work my way down the uneven aisles, careful not to walk on anything but the very narrow strip of grass that borders each straight row of graves.

And then I find it, feeling yet again the shock of his name having both a birth date and a death date. His name. And yet no him. I still find myself in a state of disbelief, that this could possibly be real – today, six years on, on what should have been his 59th birthday. That he is actually dead. So perplexing, so complex, so strange... so matter-of-fact, so ordinary, so true. The facts of someone going from alive, to dead. The demate-rialisation of a human being.

Today, as I always do, I start to tell him how much I miss him and then I stop, as there is nothing more to say. It is just too strange, to talk to someone who cannot reply. It reminds me of the moment minutes after his death when I laid my head awkwardly on his still warm bare arm, as three tired nurses stood at the head of his bed, watching. Then, too, I started to talk but became tongue-tied at the ludicrousness of doing such a thing, not least in front of strangers. I patted his arm, like a polite stranger, and left. I think I said *Bye*. Minutes later, I walked to the lift, trundling his little wheelie behind me, hastily packed. Pressed the lift button, waited, noting that the lift was taking a long time this morning, nodding to the people already in it. *Hi*. Absurd, I remember thinking. Close to funny, this is so fucking mad.

But today I wipe my cheeks and smear sudden surprising tears over my chilly face with my sleeve. I am so, so sorry. So sorry that you are dead. I end up saying. As usual, I stuff two letters the children and I have written into the small crack between the head stone and stone that covers the grave, poking them down with the others that I have left there over the last six years.

Back in the car, my father does not ask me anything but puts his hand over mine as I hold the steering wheel again.

Ok, back we go. I carefully turn the car around, noticing his kind eyes, large and blue, lined and furrowed, are edged with red and glistening.

Now, my world is a good, rich, satisfying one again. I am happy. Work is hard but engrossing, my sons are thriving, my parents remain well and I have a new love. We have a new life together. But what I know, and what the bereaved have to learn, is that the new life, once rebuilt, must be lived alongside the sadness of the loss of the old life. The experience of the death of a partner leaves a hollow behind, which is vast, cavernous and full of dark shadows that unexpectedly reveal sharp and painful objects, to trip over, and wind you. These objects are memories, which re-emerge suddenly when the loved one is dead, and are quite different to a memory of someone still alive. The de-cathexis, the letting go, is of a different texture to those ties you abandon because someone no longer loves you, or you no longer love them. When someone dies, and they still love you, there is a guilt that must also be endured in the survivor. That you have life still. Something they wanted so much too. That you can move on, and they are immobilised, stuck forever. It has nothing to do with falling in love again and everything to do with simply drawing air and being in the world still – without them.

In the most ordinary and prosaic of ways, memory haunts you differently in a photo that falls out of a book, or a letter's deeply familiar handwriting that a pen will never form again. Memory that is shared is of a different order. A widow's memory of a marriage anniversary cannot be celebrated. Was I married to Andrew for seven months, or seven years? What counts? His birthday, his yahrzeit, the day of his death? In a way, these are nothing to do with me, so I can remember, note them. But the other dates, the first time I saw him, our first lunch, supper, holiday, engagement, our wedding day...? This is much more complex. What does the memorialisation of a couple that is dead mean? Who are these private calculations, internal ruminations, reminiscences and recollections for, if they cannot be shared, and only bring pain?

Grief experts urge us to find strength, power, 'silver linings' and resilience in our experiences, but that has never been the case with me. We, most of us, choose to live on because the death instinct still eludes us, and life is there to be lived. Those who lost their partners because of Covid suffered, many of them, unspeakable trauma, and often, goodbyes mouthed only by phone or on an iPad. In some cases, there was no goodbye. We are all wondering now whether the shock of the Pandemic, will, with luck eventually blur, and become a part of a shared history.

But things are never equal, and the mass loss of life will never be felt by onlookers as it is by those bereaved. We must not forget them, nor should we look for change, improvements, smiles, new interests, relationships or love. We must let them remain in their couples, silent, alone, stunned, disbelieving. We must respect the one of two they once were, not degrade or diminish the stature of the loving state of mind they had with their lost person. Gradually, the grief ebbing away, the mourning beginning, they may start to be able to join the rest of us again, in whatever way is possible. Listen to what they need, let us not exclude or forget them. Listen to me, for I am back in the world again, no longer defined by my loss, but forever changed by his love.

London, June 2021

Acknowledgements

This is a book that took me almost five years, much of it written as events unfolded, but some much later, as I began to recover from the shock of my loss.

My understanding of Freud has developed more since I finished writing and began training as an analyst. I delved deeply into one of his seminal papers for this book, but seeking to understand his theories fully will be the enjoyable task of a lifetime, as any student of Freud soon realises.

I have used some pseudonyms to protect privacy, but these people will know who they are, and how grateful I am to them, particularly the team that cared for Andrew at Yale.

I would also like to acknowledge the importance of and how much I have learnt from all my patients, individuals and couples, past and present.

Many thanks to Aurea Carpenter, Evie Dunne, Kate Hubbard, Rebecca Nicolson and all at Short Books for their sensitivity, patience and persistence.

And my parents, Alison Soskice, David Soskice and my sons, G and F.

It could not have been written without the constant loving presence of Saydar Miranda: a huge support to all our family.

Anne Robinson helped me make this book as good as it could be. Likewise, Anji Hunter kept asking me how it was going (meaning 'get on with it'; so I did) while Fiona Millar showed me exceptional kindness in the immediate aftermath and for years afterwards which I will never forget. I could not have asked for more from my friendship with Stewart Wood or Carine Minne. Nicola Lacey, my stepmother, has been the most generous and careful reader.

My sincere gratitude for kindness over the years, with this book but in many other ways to Decca Aikenhead, Lisa Armstrong, Cathy Baker, Anna and Lucia Bastiani, Luciana Berger, Alessandra Benvenuti, Michael Brearley, Camilla Bustani, Tammy Clewell, Josh Cohen, Melanie Clore, Derek Draper, Ora Dresner, Ros Edwardes, Marika Freris, Gail Gallie, Kate Garvey, Kate Gavron, Amelia Gentleman, Richard Gordon, Tom Hammick, Hannah Hawkins, Emer Hoskin, Ian Katz, Dixie Linder, Isabelle Macphail, Andrew Matthews-Owen, Yaron Meshoulam, David Mitchell, Parry Mitchell, Hannah Lowy-Mitchell, Matthew Norman, Rhian O'Connor, Alan and Josephine Ogden, Fiona Parkin, Rachel Reeves, Justine Roberts, Jan Royall, Abigail Schama, Carey Scott, Wasi Siddiqui, Julia Simpson, the Soskice family, Rachel Speight, Phil Stokoe, Jan Toledano, Rachel Ulanet, Shriti Vadera, Matthias Von Der Tann, Ben Wegg-Prosser and Claire Wright.

I thank Rachel Cooke and Leon Kleimberg, for more than words can express.

Lastly, my love to Ben Macintyre.

Further reading

Sigmund Freud. 'Mourning and Melancholia' and 'On Transience' In: *The standard edition of the complete psychological works of Sigmund Freud* (vol 14). Strachey J (Ed and Trans). (1957). Hogarth Press, London.

G. Fichtner (Ed). 'Letter to Ludswig Binswanger April 11, 1929'. *The Sigmund Freud-Ludwig Binswanger Correspondence 1908-1938*. (2003). Other Press, New York.

Peter Gay. *Freud: A Life for Our Time* (1988). J M Dent & Sons, London.

Books

Marie Adams. *The Myth of the Untroubled Therapist* (2014). Routledge, London.

Julian Barnes. *Levels Of Life* (2014). Vintage, London.

Joan Didion. *The Year Of Magical Thinking* (2005). Alfred A Knopf, New York.

Glocer Fiorini, Bokanowski and Lewkowicz. *On Freud's 'Mourning and Melancholia'* (2007). IPA, London.

Kate Gross. *Late Fragments: Everything I Want to Tell You (About This Magnificent Life)* (2014). William Collins, London.

Paul Kalanithi. *When Breath Becomes Air* (2016). Random House, London.

Darian Leader. *The New Black: Mourning, Melancholia and Depression* (2008). Hamish Hamilton, London.

CS Lewis. *A Grief Observed* (1961). Faber and Faber, London.

Richard Lloyd Parry. *Ghosts Of The Tsunami: Death and*

Life in Japan's Disaster Zone (2017). Jonathan Cape, London.

Donald Moss. *At War With The Obvious* (2017). Routledge, London.

Mary Morgan. *A Couple State Of Mind* (2019). Routledge, London.

Charles Rycroft. *A Critical Dictionary of Psychoanalysis* (1968). Penguin, London.

Papers and Articles

Barbara Chasen. 'Death of a Psychoanalyst's Child' In: Gerson B (Ed). *The Therapist as a Person* (1996). Wiley, New York.

Tammy Clewell. 'Mourning Beyond Melancholia: Freud's Psychoanalysis Of Loss' *Journal American Psychoanalytic Association,* 52.1 (2004).

Andy Kopsa 'There Are No Five Stages Of Grief' *The New York Times* (28 February 2019).

Meghan O'Rourke 'Good Grief' *The New Yorker* (24 January 2010).

Juliet Rosenfeld is a psychotherapist and writer who works in private practice in London. After studying languages at Oxford, she spent 15 years in advertising before retraining as a clinician. She has written for a variety of publications and is especially interested in understanding the role of grief and love in the consulting room. Juliet is an elected Trustee of the UK Council of Psychotherapy, and clinical trustee of the Freud Museum London. She is currently writing her second book, 'Affairs' (to be published in 2023), which seeks to understand from a psychological perspective why people have affairs, and the childhood roots that are so often at the heart of these complex relationships.